TAKE MORE VACATIONS

TAKE MORE VACATIONS

HOW TO SEARCH BETTER, BOOK CHEAPER, AND TRAVEL THE WORLD

SCOTT KEYES

HARPER WAVE
An Imprint of HarperCollins*Publishers*

Illustration on page 209 adapted from blank map of Europe by Maix and Tintazul under CC BY-SA 3.0.

FIRST EDITION

Designed by Jamie Lynn Kerner
Charts and graphs designed by Jen Overstreet

Library of Congress Cataloging-in-Publication Data has been applied for.

ISBN 978-0-06-299354-0

21 22 23 24 25 LSC 10 9 8 7 6 5 4 3 2

CONTENTS

INTRODUCTION

IN 2013, I FLEW NONSTOP FROM NEW YORK CITY TO MI-lan on a flight that typically cost $850 roundtrip. I paid $130.

I'd never considered visiting northern Italy until the moment those fares popped up. In fact, the only thing I knew about Milan was its reputation as a fashion hub. (And trust me, nobody has ever looked at my wardrobe and thought: *Now that's a trendsetter.*)

But at $130, the question was no longer "Can I afford to go?"; it was "Do I *want* to go?"

For that price, I didn't have to give it much thought. On December 9, I boarded United Airlines Flight 19 and woke up the next morning in Italy.

The following week was a joyous blur: hiking trails forged among Cinque Terre's picturesque villages; boarding a chairlift in Italy and getting off in the Swiss Alps; feeling San Siro Stadium shake with energy during an AC Milan soccer match; staving off a food coma in Lake Como after burying my face in fresh pasta and cheeses.

If roundtrip flights had cost $850, as they typically did, I never would have gone to Milan. After all, it was a destination that hadn't even been on my travel radar a month earlier. And like most people—especially recent college grads—my meager bank account didn't allow for expensive nonstop flights to Europe.

On past vacations where I'd paid quite a bit for flights, the fare stuck with me throughout the journey, an omnipresent pressure to Get the Most Out of My Trip. Time off was supposed to be fun and liberating, yet the expense of flights left me more stressed than I was before I'd left.

Flying to Milan, though, the airfare was less a sword of Damocles, hanging overhead threatening financial ruin, and more a source of pride and freedom. The cheap fare had relieved the pressure I usually felt to make a trip's expense worth it. Nor did I have anxiety about whether I'd overpaid. I was a gambler playing with house money.

Not needing to justify expensive flights had some unexpected benefits. My mental state was looser, more relaxed, less concerned with whether I was enjoying myself enough to account for the expense of getting to Milan. My usual tight-fisted self opened up, and I indulged on better meals and drinks than I usually allowed myself. After all, I'd saved over $700 on flights, so what's an extra couple of bucks for truffle linguine or an Aperol Spritz? Expensive activities that I would've avoided on previous trips (like skiing in the Alps) were fair game. Even with lifestyle inflation, the flight savings meant I still spent less overall—and as important, I enjoyed myself more. The savings had put a halo on the entire trip.

My experience in Milan became a revelation for future trips. If I could get away with paying a fraction of the $850 and more I used to pay for flights, I could take three or four trips for less than what I'd previously paid for one. I'd be able to try out more places, spend time exploring new countries and cuisines, knowing all the while that if I found somewhere I particularly loved I could soon make it back. I could stop treating each trip as a once-in-a-lifetime opportunity.

And so I started taking chances on more off-the-beaten-path locations. There were a few flops in there, of course, but many happy surprises too: Lithuania, Trinidad and Tobago, Taiwan, and interior Mexico all wound up being some of my favorite trips. I may never have gotten to visit any of these if I'd confined myself to $850 flights—and thus one trip per year, at most—because I would've been less willing to take a gamble on somewhere unconventional.

After that serendipitous trip to Milan, word spread to coworkers and friends who all had the same request: "Scott, when you find another deal like that, can you let me know so I can get it too?" Rather than trying to remember everyone I'd promised to alert, I started a simple little email list: Scott's Cheap Flights.

Today, Scott's Cheap Flights has over two million members who have collectively saved over $500 million off normal flight prices since 2015.

It couldn't have happened but for the fact that since the mid-2010s we've been living in what I call the Golden Age of Cheap Flights. Not every single flight is inexpensive, of course, just as you couldn't sink a shovel into any random 1850s-era patch of California dirt and expect to find a gold nugget. Never in history, though, have flights been as cheap and numerous as they are today.

And yet, in 2018—as fares departing the United States dropped as low as $224 roundtrip to Paris and $377 roundtrip to Tokyo—a Morning Consult poll found that only 13 percent of respondents said the cost of flights had gotten better in the past few years. Meanwhile, 71 percent said airfare had stayed the same or gotten worse.

Though airfare can be erratic, it's not indecipherable. On the contrary, with a basic knowledge of how airfare works, anyone can relish the joy of cheap flights. That's why I set out to write this book: a manifesto for finding cheap flights so you can travel, see, live more.

Nobody wants to overpay for airfare, so why do so many of us do it? Why do we hand over $1,000 for a single roundtrip fare to Europe when that much cash could easily buy three flights? It's because plane tickets are one of the most confusing purchases we regularly make, and there's a remarkable lack of trustworthy guidance—plus a staggering amount of disinformation—on how to get good deals. After all, the airlines want you to stay baffled. It's in their financial interest. The less you know about airfare, the more you'll spend on it.

For years, we've been taught to think of airfare like most other consumer products, with predictable and stable prices. And we've internalized seemingly commonsense ideas about what flights should cost. Long flights should be expensive; short flights should be cheap. Unsold last-minute seats ought to be heavily discounted. It all makes intuitive sense.

Turns out, we're all wrong. Here's why.

Let's compare purchasing flights with buying some bagels.

When you shop for bagels, the price is essentially the same on any given day, and it mostly depends on how many you buy.

But when you shop for flights, the price is highly volatile. The same flight that costs $800 today may cost $300 tomorrow and $1,300 the next day. And the price of a flight bears little relation to how far you travel. It costs more to fly from the United States to Jamaica, for instance, than it does from the United States to China.

If you get home and realize you already had plenty of bagels, you usually can go back to the store for a full refund. Not so with airfare, unless you're prepared to pay hundreds of dollars in fees.

As unsold bagels near their expiration date, the price gets slashed. An unsold seat nearing takeoff date, meanwhile, soars in price.

Bagel prices are consistent and logical. And as anyone who's gluten intolerant will tell you, bagels are not essential. Airfare, on the other hand, is unpredictable and irrational. And if you want to travel overseas, a flight is all but required.

The fact that airfare behaves according to its own unique rules is a problem for would-be tourists. We have no idea what flight prices will or should be. We're left anxious about when to book, anxious about whether to book, and ever fearful that we'll wind up overpaying.

As airfare shifted over the past few decades from something you bought through a travel agent to something you bought for yourself online, the amount of information that travelers were expected to sift through multiplied a thousandfold. We have all the fares at our fingertips—a fire hose of possible trips—and no idea what to do with them. It's like having access to the entire Wikipedia archive, but only in Hungarian.

How much are fares to London? What do they usually cost?

Will fares go up or down if I wait a week? A month? Is it cheaper if I go later in the year? Is this airline okay? There's a short connection, will I miss my flight? What then? Do I have to pay for luggage? What if I need to change my ticket?

A huckster industry has entered this void over the years, claiming various "hacks" that will guarantee cheap flights. Book your flights Tuesday at 1 p.m. Clear your cookies. Wait until the last minute to book. X Airline or Y Online Travel Agency always has the cheapest fares. Fares are 5 percent more expensive this year than last year. Flights are always cheapest 70 days before departure.

At best, this advice is misleading; at worst, it's incorrect and counterproductive.

Finding cheap flights isn't about tactics like coupon codes or browsing in incognito mode; finding cheap flights is about strategy. It's about rethinking how you search.

Paradoxically, studies have found that for most people, planning a trip is both the happiest and most stressful part of travel. Anticipation is a hell of a drug: Think how much fun that trip to South Africa will be! But the confusion of planning a trip and booking flights acts as a mental tax of sorts, eating away at what's supposed to be a joyous activity. Just as overpaying for flights erodes the joy of travel, so too does the uncertainty—not knowing when you ought to book, what you should expect to pay for flights, what's a good deal, and how likely are cheap flights to pop up.

But what if the planning process, instead of being stressful and anxiety inducing, were as fun as the trip itself? What if, instead of dreading booking flights, we looked forward to it?

A funny thing happens when you book an unexpectedly

cheap flight: It transforms the act of handing over money from a reluctant experience to an exuberant one. I was *excited* to pay for that $130 Milan flight in a way I never would have been with an $850 flight, even though it would have been the exact same trip.

Travel is not just for the rich. The era of talking about flying overseas in hushed and revered tones, as if it's an indulgence reserved for the aristocracy, is over. Nor is international travel just for people flying out of big cities. In fact, I'll show you why, counter to public perception, smaller airports (think Fargo, Portland, Columbus) get the best deals.

I'll explain why flights have gotten cheaper over the years and share methods of searching to get the best deals. I'll answer persistent questions of when and where to book flights, and dispel various flight-booking myths that have popped up over the years.

We'll dive into mistake fares—the holy grail of cheap flights—and why airlines honor tickets they mistakenly sold for over 90 percent off normal prices. You'll learn one of the surprising best weeks of the year to travel, why budget airlines are great for you even if you never fly one, and how the most expensive mistake we make when booking flights is choosing a trip rather than choosing a fare.

Changing the way you think about buying flights isn't easy. The good news is that once you've learned what this book has to teach, trips that had been unthinkable become possible. Vacations transform from an annual indulgence to one enjoyed three times per year. Bucket lists get tackled before retirement. You become that person in your friend group who is always traveling, leaving everyone else to wonder how you do it.

Cheap flights don't just save money; they make the world smaller and more accessible. They offer vacations that are more fun and less pressure-laden because you know you got a deal. Cheap flights transform you during your trip and, as important, after you get back. They leave you a happier, more fulfilled, and more worldly person than you were before you left.

TAKE MORE VACATIONS

YOU DON'T TAKE ENOUGH VACATION: THE CURSE OF EXPENSIVE FLIGHTS

CHANCES ARE, YOU'D LIKE TO TAKE MORE TRIPS THAN you actually do.

Travel is consistently a top New Year's resolution. It's the #1 activity people say they plan to do as they get older. It gets better ratings than sex. Unlike some hobbies—say, bike polo or knitting—that have limited appeal, travel is an incredibly popular activity.

Although we say we want to take more trips, in practice we're taking fewer. From 1978 to 2000, Americans took 20 vacation days a year on average. By 2014, though, that number had fallen to just 16. Currently, more than half of all employees nationwide don't use all of their paid time off, leaving 768 million days unused each year.

This dissonance—our wanting to travel more than we actually do—is especially true among millennials. A 2016 Airbnb poll found that millennials say traveling is more important than saving for a house, buying a car, or paying down debt. And yet we take the least vacation time of any generation, just 14.5 days in 2017—16 percent less than the average American and 26 percent less than baby boomers.

What's going on here?

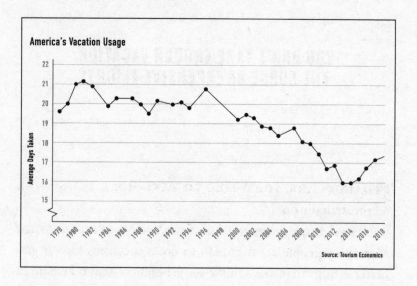

One possibility is not enough vacation time. The United States is the only advanced economy—and one of the few nations worldwide—that doesn't guarantee workers any paid leave. Though the average American worker receives 23 paid days off per year, for many that number is far less, or even zero. And even those with paid time off often have travel obligations—visiting family, friends' weddings, reunions—that crowd out time they'd otherwise use for vacation.

But paid vacation time is no guarantee of more vacations. While some people do run out of vacation days, the fact remains that most people don't, perhaps fearful that their boss would view them as a flake or underachiever. We're currently on pace for one billion unused vacation days by the end of 2021. Sufficient time is *a* reason, not *the* reason, we don't travel more.

I suspect that what's holding us back instead is the misery of booking flights. For as much as we bemoan long flights or travel mishaps, the biggest source of vacation stress is buying the ticket and planning the trip.

WHY WE LOVE TRAVEL
BUT HATE TRAVEL PLANNING

When does a trip become real? It's not when you're first thinking about going somewhere. We daydream about travel every time we open up Instagram or watch Anthony Bourdain. It's not when you mentally decide to go somewhere, either. You could still change your mind, especially if airfare is outrageous.

Instead, a trip becomes real the moment you book your flight. Before that, it's an idea; after, it's a plan. It's happening.

Although we can't start relishing an upcoming trip until the flight is secured, it's that booking stage where so many of us find ourselves stuck. We get caught in limbo, watching prices alternate between expensive and extortionate, helpless to do anything about it.

In 2012, researchers from the College of Charleston and Austria's MCI Management Center Innsbruck conducted a study to find where travelers felt the most stress in the course of a trip. "The results were somewhat surprising," the authors wrote. Much maligned sources of vacation stress—from packing to flight delays to bad weather to spending hours in a cramped plane—paled in comparison to what turned out to be the biggest stressor: planning.

What part of the trip-planning process is exhausting us? It's not hiring a dog sitter or figuring out what to do in Cartagena. "Developing the [vacation] itinerary . . . as well as making arrangements to be away from one's work and home generated the lowest amount of stress," researchers found. Instead, it's the expense and difficulty of planning travel logistics that's causing anguish. Not knowing when to get flights, where to book, whether you're a savant or a sucker paying that much for a flight to Colombia.

The cost, volatility, and complexity of booking flights adds anxiety to an already-uncertain process. Few among us enjoy searching for flights, watching fares bop around seemingly at random. Everybody fears overpaying, and with little understanding about how airfare will behave, it's a high-stakes game of Whac-A-Mole.

In our minds, travel is supposed to be fun and relaxing. But booking flights is anything but fun and relaxing. The result of that expectations mismatch? Tension.

In some cases, the stress of planning and the cost of flights can be so extreme as to completely cancel out the joy of travel. A 2013 study from Harvard University and the Institute for Applied Positive Research found that the uncertainty of planning could actually negate the mental benefits of a vacation. According to the researchers, "Most of the happiness gleaned from vacation is dependent upon the stress level of the vacation. Poorly planned and stressful vacations eliminate the positive benefit of time away."

Planning international trips in particular can wreak havoc on travelers' mental well-being. Researchers found that, compared to domestic travel, planning an international trip was twice as likely to cause stress. One reason: If you want to travel overseas, opting out of airfare isn't an option. You can't take a road trip from New York to Paris. And if you pay inflated prices, flights to France can get a lot more expensive than flights to Chicago.

Of course, one way to avoid extra stress is by traveling only domestically, but come on, that's a terrible solution. It makes as much sense as a skier never getting off the bunny hill, lest she risk falling down. Instead, the better option is to improve your skill set so you can go anywhere without overwhelming stress.

Though some may argue that planning is inherently menial at best and excruciating at worst, that's only true when it's done poorly. Once you've mastered airfare, travel planning will transform from one of the worst parts of a trip to one of the best. What's more, it'll help you travel more and better. Planners, according to a 2019 survey from the U.S. Travel Association, were 50 percent happier than nonplanners in both how much they enjoyed their vacations and how much time off they took.

I too used to hate booking flights. I overpaid all the time and drove myself crazy guessing whether a flight I wanted would go up in price or down, unsure if it would ever drop to a level I'd consider "cheap."

Nowadays I genuinely love booking trips—it's the same energy as a kid opening presents—but only because I'm buying $130 roundtrip flights to Italy and $169 roundtrip to Japan. I sure as hell wouldn't have fun paying $1,300 for those same tickets. After so many years of overpaying for flights, it's a great feeling getting a win over the airlines.

Although airfare is no longer the most uniquely torturous

item I regularly purchase, for many people it still is. What if you could conquer that mental load stopping you from taking more vacations? It's natural to think of stress as an intrinsic part of the planning process, but what if it weren't? If flights were cheap, and you felt confident when booking them, would you travel more?

Everyone is capable of overcoming the planning agony and turning airfare into a joy rather than a burden. But to do so, it's helpful to first understand the psychology and cognitive tendencies that prompt us to pay too much for flights.

WHY WE BOOK EXPENSIVE FLIGHTS

Oftentimes when I get into discussions of airfare, someone will sheepishly divulge that they recently overpaid for a flight.

Take my coworker Katie's 2008 Argentina trip to celebrate her husband's birthday. When she first started looking at fares out of Chicago, they were $700 apiece. Not terrible for Buenos Aires, where flights are notoriously expensive, but it was more money than she had lying around, especially for two tickets. By the time a few more paychecks came in and she was ready to buy, fares had gone up to $900. A bitter pill, but she resigned herself to booking. When she went to complete the purchase, though, she was given a rude surprise: The price had jumped to $1,600 each.

"I remember being so upset that I'd missed the window to get the tickets at a good price and I was thinking I'd have to totally change this surprise trip to a different destination," she said. Katie monitored prices each morning for the next two weeks, anxious over every movement. When fares finally dropped to $800, she booked right away, worried that they'd instantaneously go up again. After months of stress watching flights, she finally had her tickets, even if it felt like a Pyrrhic victory. "I still overpaid," she said.

Expensive flights can feel like a failure. And divulging the fare can feel humiliating, as though overpaying for flights means you're a sucker who didn't know any better.

To be clear, there's nothing shameful per se about overpaying. Paying too much is just an accidental byproduct. People don't set out to book expensive flights; people wind up booking expensive flights.

So why do we do it?

Sometimes better flights are just more expensive. A nonstop flight may cost more than a connecting flight. Red-eyes may be cheaper than a daytime flight. We pay more for superior service.

But we don't always get a better flight by paying more. On your next flight, ask your seatmates what they paid. (It can be a surprisingly fun exercise, truly! Just keep the humblebragging to a minimum if you got an amazing fare.) You'll often find a variation of $1,000 or more.

Let's use an example: a roundtrip flight from Austin to Tokyo. Priya sitting in seat 31A paid $500, while Tom sitting in 31B paid $1,500. What drove Tom to pay three times as much as Priya?

It could have been convenience. Perhaps Tom had plenty of money and didn't want to spend much time or effort monitoring airfare. When Orbitz told him that flights to Japan were $1,500, he decided that was an acceptable fare. It's not that Tom wouldn't have preferred to pay less, but he balked at the notion of spending additional energy hunting for a better deal. He had better things to do.

We don't all have $1,500 lying around for flights like Tom. For Priya, the ticket price wasn't a convenience; it was the difference between getting to visit Japan or not. Many more people can afford $500 flights than can afford $1,500 flights, especially if they're buying multiple tickets. Cheap flights aren't always optional.

There's a more likely explanation for why Tom, against his preference, paid three times what his seatmate did: human psychology.

Cognitive biases—the basis of behavioral economics, which explores why humans act in predictably irrational ways—impact every part of our lives, and booking flights is no exception. Understanding the psychological tendencies that push us to book bad fares is the first step to overcoming them.

Here are some of the mental biases to which we fall prey when purchasing airfare:

Loss Aversion: For many of us, the joy we feel when fares go down pales in comparison to the angst we feel when fares go up. This is called loss aversion. "Losses hurt about twice as much as gains make us feel good," Nobel Prize–winning economist Richard Thaler has argued. By this calculation, a flight currently selling for $1,500 would have to drop to $500 for us to have the same intensity of feeling as when it rises to $2,000. Because fares going up feel bad more than fares going down feel good, booking mediocre flights today can feel preferable to gambling on what prices will be tomorrow. Given the unpredictability of airfare, perhaps Tom booked a $1,500 Japan flight as a defense mechanism because he feared it would go up past $2,000.

Anchoring: If you're flying somewhere you've visited before, the fare you paid last time may anchor your perception of what fares "should" be today. When Tom visited Japan a decade ago, he paid $1,400. An extra $100 this time feels reasonable enough, especially considering inflation. What he's ignoring, of course, is the broader overall trend in airfare. Before 2010, it was nearly unheard of to see Austin–Tokyo flights under $1,200 roundtrip. By 2019, that route was dropping below $600 roundtrip at least a few times a year, and sometimes lower. Tom's previous trip anchored his expectations higher than they should've been. He didn't hold out for the fares Priya got because he didn't think they could exist.

Recency Bias: Say Tom searched for airfare from Austin to Tokyo every day for a month. For thirty days straight, the fare was close to the long-term average for the route, around $1,200 roundtrip. After monitoring flights for more than four weeks and seeing a more or less static fare, he may have gotten antsy to book because he assumed the fare was unlikely to drop. This is recency bias, relying solely on recent experience to guide decision making. But, like a turkey who's been well fed leading up to Thanksgiving and has little reason to think anything will change, Tom had no way of knowing that Tokyo flights would drop to $500 roundtrip on Day 31. Similar to anchoring, recency bias had narrowed Tom's expectations, blinding him to the reality that Tokyo flights would soon be deeply discounted.

Sunk Cost Fallacy: The most common way in which people plan vacations is to decide where and when they want to travel, and only later do they consider the fares. (More on the fallacy of this approach and a superior strategy in Chapter 3.) Once we've mentally committed ourselves to a specific trip, not going or going somewhere else doesn't feel like an option. This is the sunk cost fallacy at work, a phenomenon whereby we continue doing something solely because we've already invested a lot of time or effort in it. Tom spent months planning his trip to Tokyo before he started looking at airfare. By that point, he was so attached to Japan that he didn't entertain the idea of traveling elsewhere, even if $500 roundtrip flights to Vietnam popped up. He was committed to Japan, so he was committed to airfare to Japan, regardless of whether ticket prices dropped.

Wishful Thinking: Our desire for something to be true often outweighs an objective analysis of whether something actually is true. For example, many people want it to be the case that airlines slash fares on last-minute empty seats, despite the fact that for decades airlines have jacked up prices on last-minute fares. Tom may have waited to book until a week or two before his flight because his hope that cheap fares would pop up late clouded an objective examination of whether they actually would. (They wouldn't.)

Procrastination: Tom may have booked fares too late—and paid too much as a result—for the same reason students cram before a final. Like studying, booking flights is few people's idea of a good time. (It is my idea of a good time, but I recognize this is an outlier belief.) What do we do with necessary but unpleasant tasks? We procrastinate. We put them off. But as with wishful thinking, if the temptation to put off distasteful chores results in booking flights at the last minute, we're resigning ourselves to expensive flights in the process.

It's almost always possible to avoid expensive flights. Prevention requires not only a strong grasp of the cheap-flight-finding strategies I'm going to teach you but also awareness of the cognitive biases that push us, against our better judgment, to overpay.

However, there are times expensive flights are unavoidable. If your grandma is in hospice with days to live, your flight options are quite limited. Some of the normal tools in our arsenal to find cheaper flights—waiting for the fare to drop, flying into or out of different airports, changing your travel dates—aren't worth it when time is of the essence.

9 STRATEGIES WHEN YOU DON'T HAVE FLEXIBILITY

1. Check fares out of close, drivable airports.
2. Check fares from nearby major hubs, like LAX or JFK. If they're hundreds cheaper, take a short positioning flight.
3. Check fares to airports near where you're going and get to your final destination by train, bus, or short budget flight.

4. Check if flying out a few days earlier or flying back a few days later will be significantly cheaper.

5. Even if you have zero flexibility on dates, check a day before or after in case there are, say, red-eye flights just past midnight.

6. Start searching as early as possible.

7. Don't wait until the last minute to book. Flights will get more expensive in the final three weeks, not cheaper.

8. Check Skiplagged.com for hidden-city tickets.

9. If you've got a stash of frequent flyer miles, see if there are any cheap award flights.

Thankfully, few of our trips are in such dire circumstances. Most of the time, we have a multitude of options to find cheaper fares. Whether we take advantage of them is up to us.

KEY TAKEAWAYS

- Most of us want to travel more than we actually do, but the uncertainty of planning trips and booking flights stops us from taking more vacations. In some cases, planning stress can outweigh the mental benefits of going on a trip.

- Airfare can be expensive, volatile, and unpredictable. The fact that we need flights for most vacations makes it a uniquely agonizing purchase.

- Subliminal cognitive biases are pushing us to over-pay for tickets. Though in theory we'd all prefer cheap flights, in practice susceptibilities like loss aversion and procrastination unintentionally drive us to book expensive flights.

2

TRAVEL AS MEDICINE:
HOW CHEAP FLIGHTS LEAD TO HAPPIER TRIPS (AND MORE OF THEM)

NEARLY EVERY FACET OF MODERN SOCIETY, EVEN THE traditionally popular stuff, is up for debate nowadays. Some people loathe bikes and others (including me) dislike fruit pie. Dogs somehow have haters, and ice cream is downright controversial. Hot takes and contrarian trolls are everywhere.

Yet through it all, travel remains beloved. If anything, travel's popularity is increasing, and it's not just short weekend trips. In 2018, more than 93 million Americans traveled abroad, a 47 percent increase in five years. To the extent travel elicits debate, it's because it's *too* popular. Everyone wants to visit Paris, how will we all fit?

What is it about travel that's so appealing? Why do we pay good chunks of money to leave our homes for strange, foreign lands? To leave our comfortable beds and adorable pets for anonymous hotel rooms half a world away? To ditch our friends and spend time among strangers, to leave the known for the unknown?

There's a simple explanation for why you want to get away: Travel is good for you. Survey after survey shows that travelers are happier, healthier, and more productive than nontravelers.

A 2018 poll of more than four thousand American full-time workers looked at how "mega-travelers" (people who used all or most of their vacation days to travel) compared in well-being with "homebodies," who used little or none of their time off to travel.

Across the board, researchers from the U.S. Travel Association found that mega-travelers were significantly better off than their homebody counterparts. For instance:

- 79 percent of mega-travelers reported being happy in their relationships versus 66 percent of homebodies.
- 76 percent of mega-travelers enjoyed their time off versus 48 percent of homebodies.
- 61 percent of mega-travelers were happy with their health and physical well-being versus 39 percent of homebodies.
- 59 percent of mega-travelers liked their place of employment versus 46 percent of homebodies.
- 57 percent of mega-travelers liked their job versus 46 percent of homebodies.
- 52 percent of mega-travelers got promoted in the last two years versus 44 percent of homebodies.

Researchers have found other ways travel can impact your life as well, including:

- It improves your mood even more than exercising or shopping.
- It makes you more employable and better equipped to make big life decisions.
- It lowers your risk of heart disease and depression.

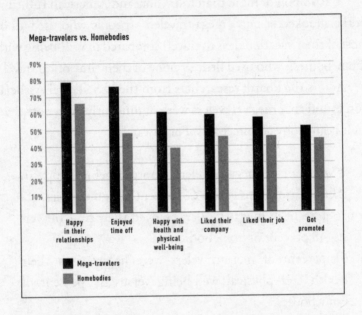

A small percentage of people even reported weight loss, improved skin, and an uptick in their sex drive.

Travel isn't just correlated with better life outcomes; it's helping promote them. "Traveling can help reduce the levels of the stress hormone cortisol," said Dr. Linda Papadopoulos, a Canadian psychologist who worked with Expedia on a major 2017 study of travelers. "As stress and anxiety decreases, mood increases—bringing many, often unexpected, positive benefits in how we perceive ourselves, motivation and productivity, and our general outlook on life."

Dr. Paul D. Nussbaum, a clinical neuropsychologist at the University of Pittsburgh School of Medicine, put it even more bluntly: "Travel is good medicine." By "challeng[ing] the brain with new and different experiences and environments," Nussbaum argued, travel "promotes brain health and builds brain resilience across the lifespan."

In fact, there's an emerging body of research showing that spending money on experiences—like travel—tends to boost happiness more than spending money on possessions. A 2010 study conducted by academics at the University of Wisconsin and University of Chicago, for instance, found that of nine major categories of spending, the only one positively related to happiness was leisure spending, like travel.

There are many reasons why experiential spending tends to boost happiness more than material spending. Unlike buying things, which we quickly grow accustomed to, experiences are a perpetual joy. We're far more likely to mentally revisit experiences, use them to define our identity, and share them with others, according to a 2003 University of Colorado and Cornell University study. There's a quote popularly attributed to Theodore Roosevelt that "comparison is the thief of joy," but unlike material things, experiences don't lend themselves well to comparison. A BMW owner's joy may be diminished when he drives alongside a Maserati, but your backpacking trip in Patagonia in no way diminishes my Oktoberfest adventure in Germany. Hiking in the mountains and drinking in beer halls are both fun activities; the fact that they can't be compared on an apples-to-apples basis means that we can discuss our respective trips and neither traveler is made to feel inferior.

This multitude of personal benefits, taken together, can be

thought of as the soft power of travel. Soft power, as described by James Fallows in his book *China Airborne*, is "when people imagine themselves transformed, improved, by adopting a new style."

Travel's enduring popularity is that soft power. Even if it's impossible to know precisely what it feels like to overlook Machu Picchu before going there, it's not hard to *imagine* how you'll feel. Nor is it unreasonable to predict that you'll love it and come back fulfilled, considering that 93 percent of travelers report feeling happier after a vacation than before. Few travelers regret the trips they took, and it's understandable why: They return happier, healthier, and better off than when they left.

The medicinal benefits of travel aren't one-and-done. Travel isn't a surgical fix; it's medicine that's best enjoyed regularly. But given that we all have limited time and funds, what's the best way to parse out our vacation time? How often—and for how long—should we go?

THE HAPPIEST WAY TO TRAVEL

Let's say you work in an office that gives you three weeks of vacation per year. How should you split up that time to generate the most happiness?

One school of thought is to use all your time off on a single big, long trip. Spend three weeks meandering around South America or Southeast Asia because an extended amount of time is the best way to get to know a place.

Advocates of "slow travel" will point to a few justifications. First, it's expensive to fly overseas, so taking one long trip means purchasing only one roundtrip flight. Second, it's lengthy and exhausting to fly internationally, not to mention jet lag. If you're going to fly all that way, a longer trip maximizes the ratio of time on the ground to time in transit. Third, a long trip is the best way to relax and experience a place beyond just surface level.

Let's examine these ideas individually. First, while expensive flights are certainly prevalent, we'll explore in Chapter 3 why they're a choice, not a requirement. We are living in the Golden Age of Cheap Flights; it's never been less expensive to travel overseas than it is today. Even a decade ago, flights to Europe under $1,000 roundtrip were rare, but now they're regularly available under $400 roundtrip. Like a form of travel inflation, taking three trips abroad in 2021 is akin to taking one overseas trip in 2011.

The second idea of maximizing vacation time to transit time is the most defensible. Nobody would argue that flying to Thailand for a one-day vacation is a good use of time, after all. However, what's harder to defend is the notion that people should wait 49 weeks between vacations. Once a relaxing three-week vacation has ended, it's a long, vacation-less slog waiting for your next trip.

What about the argument that traveling slowly is the best way to relax and absorb your surroundings? For many people it is. But slow travel isn't a free lunch. For people who have a limited amount of vacation time, slow travel means fewer trips. It's putting all your eggs in one basket. If you've got three weeks of vacation and you use it all on a trip to Fiji, what happens if by Day 3 you decide you don't much like Fiji? You may wish you had tested it with a shorter trip first. Like investment portfolios, there's value in diversifying your travels.

Even the very notion that longer vacations are more relaxing is worth questioning. In 2013, Dutch researchers at Radboud University in Nijmegen published a study examining trip length and vacationers' health and well-being. They surveyed travelers on longer vacations, 23 days on average, and found that well-being peaked on Day 8 and declined thereafter. There was no afterglow effect on individuals following a trip, as their health and wellness ratings reverted to pre-vacation levels within a week of return. "Frequent respites might be more important to preserve well-being than the duration of one single [vacation]," the authors concluded. Three one-week vacations may do us more good than one three-week vacation.

Vacations, like many parts of life, have diminishing marginal utility. To understand why, let's think of ice cream.

Imagine you're eight years old and your mom tells you that for your birthday week, you can have three scoops of ice cream, divvied up however you want. Should you get one cone with three scoops? Or three one-scoop cones spread out over the week?

Some kids will go for three scoops at once. The temptation is hard to resist, and that waffle cone is wonderful. At first. A few minutes in, though, they slowly get used to the experience. It loses some of its initial punch. By the third scoop they've got a stomachache.

The kids who decide to space their scoops out, meanwhile, understand that ice cream three days a week results in three times the anticipation. Spreading them out means enjoying them more. Plus, with just one scoop to savor each time, they never become immune to the wonderful taste.

It's not just ice cream. A 2008 New York University study looked at how interruptions impact a variety of different experiences, with some surprising results. People say they prefer positive experiences to be uninterrupted, rather than be separated by, say, a workday in the middle of a vacation. To test whether our expressed preferences line up with our revealed preferences, researchers asked subjects about to receive a massage if they would rather it be continuous or broken up into two sections. As predicted, the vast majority said they preferred a continuous massage. But when researchers put subjects into two groups, one receiving a continuous massage and one with a short break in the middle, the latter group reported significantly more pleasure from the experience. In fact, they were willing to pay nearly twice as much for the experience as respondents who had had a continuous massage.

"People are completely mispredicting when breaking up an experience would benefit them," the researchers found. It seems that just the mere act of interrupting happy experiences gives us joy because it stifles our natural inclination to get used to an experience. The interruption forces us to realize what we've adapted to and resets our excitement to experience it all over again. Parsing out positive experiences, whether it's a massage or your vacation time, is a simple way to generate more overall happiness.

Another way to get more out of your adventures is to completely ignore that old saw about quality being more important than quantity. Contrary to popular belief, researchers have found that the frequency of pleasurable experiences is more important for your well-being than quality. To understand why, consider the idea of "hedonic adaptation." This is the idea that an individual's overall happiness reverts to baseline levels even after major shocks like losing a limb or winning the lottery. A three-week vacation isn't three times better than a one-week vacation because our baseline resets not long into the trip.

However, there's a loophole to hedonic adaptation: brief, repeated events. A 2008 study from researchers at MIT, Harvard, and Duke found that the best way to improve well-being is by "shifting focus from the impact of major life changes . . . to the impact of seemingly minor repeated behaviors." For example, while it's no shock that going to a yoga class provided a small happiness boost that subsequently wore off, what the study found is that every subsequent class had the same impact. Each time a participant went, she became happier; there was no hedonic adaptation. Applying these findings to travel, it's easy to see why three shorter trips will do more for your well-being than one long vacation.

As important as how we spend our time is how we spend our money. In a seminal 2011 paper, "If Money Doesn't Make You Happy Then You Probably Aren't Spending It Right," researchers from Harvard, the University of Virginia, and the University of British Columbia examined how to stop, or at least slow, hedonic adaptation. It's not a matter of having more wealth; even a queen gets used to her riches. Instead, it's about consciously spending your money in ways that will increase personal happiness. The study's first recommendation is to buy more experiences and fewer things. "Because frequent small pleasures are different each time they occur, they forestall adaptation," the authors wrote. Each time you have an experience, even nominally similar ones like grabbing a drink with friends, it's unique. After all, the stories, the atmosphere, the circumstances are always different.

It's the same with vacations: They may be similar but they're never the same. Your trip this spring to Peru doesn't make your fall trip to New Zealand any less exciting. On the contrary, making it a priority to take frequent trips will go a long way toward boosting your well-being. To understand why, let's check in on our friends from Chapter 1, Tom and Priya.

SHORT, CHEAP FLIGHTS
OPEN UP THE WORLD

It's a new year and new you for Tom and Priya, and wouldn't you know, they made the same resolution: to travel more. They both face high housing costs and student loan debt, but each was able to set aside $1,000 for vacation flights this year. However, how they used that $1,000 to pursue their shared goal couldn't be more different.

Tom set his heart on one specific trip: early summer in London. He didn't leave his options open about where or when to go, putting all his eggs in a British summer basket instead. When he first started searching for airfare in March, flights were $900 roundtrip. Not wanting to blow all his flight money, he held out, hoping fares would come down. He waited, they didn't; he waited some more, and they remained high. Finally, he decided to just rip the bandage off one May afternoon and wound up dropping his entire $1,000 flight budget on a single roundtrip ticket.

As for the vacation itself, it went reasonably well. He liked the food, disliked the warm beer, was awed by the British Museum, and felt kind of tense throughout because of the high cost of everything. Overall, a B+ trip.

Priya, meanwhile, was intent on visiting multiple countries rather than just one. She hoped to stretch her $1,000 flight budget as much as she could. So rather than deciding on her vacation destination first, ticket prices be damned, she used the strategies laid out in this book to find cheap flights.

Pretty soon, she came across her first great deal: $320 roundtrip to Hawaii. With hardly a second thought, she booked. I mean, it's Hawaii. A month later, before she'd even left for Hawaii, Priya opened her inbox to an alert about $200 roundtrip flights to Guatemala. She'd never considered visiting Guatemala, but that's a damn cheap flight. After a few texts with her partner, they booked a week in Guatemala City and Tikal.

Later that year, while Priya was lying on the beach in Hawaii, she decided to see, just for fun, what ticket prices to Southeast Asia looked like. Vietnam and Malaysia were expensive at the time, but flights to Thailand were as low as $460 roundtrip in the fall. With $480 left in her flight budget, it felt like an omen, and pretty soon she'd booked her third trip of the year.

Priya had a great time relaxing on the beach in Hawaii, and an even better time adventuring in Guatemala. The country turned out to be a real hidden gem, in her mind, somewhere incredibly vibrant and outdoorsy, without throngs of tourists or expensive cost of living. Bangkok, on the other hand, didn't jibe with her. She loved the food and energy, but the air pollution was difficult to deal with and she wound up in an urgent care clinic after falling ill.

Let's take stock of Tom and Priya's vacations. What happens when you go Tom's route and blow your entire budget on one yearly trip? The implications are far reaching, from where you go to how you enjoy it to how you feel in between trips.

Taking one vacation a year elevates the importance of that trip. I mean, if it's your one chance to go somewhere, the stakes are high. So where do you go? Traditional tourist favorites, the big hits: Paris, Tokyo, Sydney, London. They may be crowded and expensive, but with one trip per year, you can't risk going somewhere off the beaten path. What if it sucks?

If instead you follow Priya's lead and aim for three trips a year instead of one, you can visit places further down your list, or ones you'd never even considered. With multiple trips, any one risk is less risky, and the payout is potentially much larger. By testing out different destinations, you can figure out which places jibe with you personally, rather than which places are most likely to jibe with the *average* tourist. You can take a risk on Latvia or Togo or Laos, places that aren't widely popular but are adored by some. Best case: You find a hidden gem and fall in love, like Priya did with Guatemala. Worst case: The vacation is a dud, as Bangkok was, and you get busy planning your next adventure in a few months.

The quantity of trips can also impact your vacation mindset. Because Tom knows it's his one travel opportunity of the year, he's under a good deal of self-imposed pressure to make the most of it. Maybe he's tired after a morning sightseeing around Piccadilly Circus, but to spend the afternoon relaxing in the hotel would be a waste of precious, limited vacation time. What was supposed to be a break from life's demands can easily turn into an obligation of its own. It's exhausting.

If you know you have more travel coming up soon, like Priya, you can take a more relaxed approach. You can be more charitable to yourself and any traveling companions once you stop feeling the need to always be going at full speed. Vacations become carefree adventures again.

Think of it like the weekend. Some weekends you have a lot of energy to go out, and others you just want to unwind. You know there's no need to put too much pressure on yourself to squeeze every drop out of every Saturday, because if you don't make it out this weekend, that's okay—next weekend is right around the corner. So it is with the cheap flight mindset. If you prioritize frequent short escapes, there'll be no need to sweat every minute of every trip because the next vacation is always coming up soon.

The frequency of your trips even has an impact on your well-being after you've returned home. When Tom got back from London, with no money left in his flight budget, he knew it'd be a year until his next vacation. A long, dreaded wait. In the meantime, there was little escape from the day-to-day drudgery. For Priya, though, taking a trip every four months or so meant the vacation excitement cycle could begin as soon as she got back home. While Tom was pitying himself for how long it would be until his next trip, Priya was busy planning hers.

HOW SAVING MONEY ON FLIGHTS CHANGES YOUR TRIP

Cheap flights don't just let you travel more; they also let you travel better. For some people saving on flights means better dinners and fancier cocktails, but for others it means finally living out childhood dreams.

To say Chandra Miller and her twin sister were obsessed with Disney's *Beauty and the Beast* doesn't truly capture the fanaticism. They'd watched and rewatched the movie so many times growing up they could quote every single line. They decorated their bedroom floor-to-ceiling in *Beauty and the Beast* regalia. They had the *Beauty and the Beast* Tiger Electronics handheld game, because that was a thing in the 1990s. "We were deep into it," she recounted.

Growing up, they'd always dreamed of visiting the small Alsatian villages on the French-German border that had inspired the movie's animators. Finding affordable flights from California to France was a challenge, though, and so for decades it remained a someday-maybe idea.

That someday came in 2019 when an email popped into Chandra's inbox about $356 roundtrip flights from San Francisco to Paris, including checked bags and advance seat selection. This was at least $500 off prices she'd typically seen. "I pretty much bought them within half an hour of getting the email," Chandra said. Her next order of business: recruiting her sister and their husbands to join. At $356, there wasn't much convincing needed. They had all woken up that morning with no plans for a vacation, but before lunch they had four roundtrip tickets to France, under $1,500 total.

The thing about saving so much money on flights is that it flips the mentality of making a purchase. When flights are expensive, the act of handing over money is filled with resignation. As we discussed earlier, it's a dreadful experience. When flights are cheap, though, the act of handing over money is a joyous feeling. The price alone takes the act of purchasing flights from something painful to something exciting.

As Scott's Cheap Flights member Courtney Foster wrote me in an email, "I'm not sure what I enjoyed more—the trip itself or saving so much money."

It's not just that saving money on flights leaves more in your bank account. When you get a cheap flight, it has a halo effect on your mood for the entire trip. Everything becomes glass half-full, because you don't have the nagging dread that comes from overpaying.

For example, in 2018 there was an incredible business class mistake fare from California to Southeast Asia, everywhere from Bangkok to Bali to Vietnam. Tickets that normally sold for $5,000 were suddenly available for $560 roundtrip. Thousands of Scott's Cheap Flights members—including a handful of my coworkers—got the deal before it disappeared a few hours later. After their trip, I asked those who had bought a seat to imagine how it would have been had they taken the exact same flight and done the exact same activities but paid $5,000 for their flight instead of $560. Would they have enjoyed themselves as much? The answer was the same each time: Not even close. Cheap flights made the trip way more fun.

That was precisely the experience for Chandra and her group after saving $500 a person off normal flight prices. "There wasn't any of this thinking that maybe we shouldn't go out this night because flights were so expensive," she said. "So it just opened up an extra opportunity for us to do things that we might have thought we'd have to pinch pennies on."

One of those extra opportunities: hopping on a train to visit the Alsatian villages that she and her sister had grown up dreaming about while watching *Beauty and the Beast*. Because they'd saved so much on airfare, they treated themselves to first class train tickets throughout the 10-day adventure, including a side trip to Switzerland. A splurge for sure, but one they could now afford. "It was definitely worth it," she recounted.

What would the trip have looked like if flights had cost $850? I asked. "We'd probably have to have done a shorter trip and only stayed in Paris," Chandra said. "But the highlight was everywhere else but Paris."

KEY TAKEAWAYS

- Travel is good medicine. Frequent travelers are healthier, happier, and more professionally successful than people who rarely travel.
- Frequent short trips boost your well-being more than one long trip. They let you visit more places, ensure you savor vacation rather than get used to it, and give you more anticipation because the next trip is always coming up soon.
- Cheap flights alleviate the pressure to be overly frugal during the trip itself and let you do more on your vacation than if you'd overpaid for airfare.

3

THE FLIGHT FIRST METHOD: A BETTER WAY TO SEARCH

I GOT AN EMAIL FROM MY FRIEND JULIE THE OTHER DAY:

> Hey Scott! Hope you're doing well. I was looking at a vacation to Vienna August 24–31. Any thoughts on how I can get the best price?

Since I started Scott's Cheap Flights, this is one of the most common questions I'm asked: Someone plans out a vacation, chooses the dates, and then wonders how to get the cheapest flight.

It's not a bad question per se, but it is a difficult one to answer because it rests on a flawed premise. Julie selected her destination, picked her preferred dates, and assumed she could then apply some magic salve to bring fares down. In reality, by first choosing precisely where and when she would go, Julie had inadvertently forfeited much of her ability to get cheap flights. She may as well have declared her intention to buy a new Bentley this summer, then asked how she could do so without spending much money.

Like most of us, Julie used a three-step search process to find flights I call the Destination First Method:

Step 1: Pick where you want to travel.
Step 2: Pick when you want to travel.
Step 3: Check the price.

Intentionally or not, Julie set price as the *least* important priority. She considered how much flights would cost only after settling on where she'd visit and when she'd go.

Julie's not alone. Most of us plan our vacations this way. We search flights to a specific destination for a specific week, see exorbitant fares, and wonder why the hell airfare is so expensive. It's a natural way of planning vacations. But if you're hoping for cheap flights, it's suboptimal at best and counterproductive at worst.

Fortunately, there's a better way, and it's elegantly simple: Make cheap flights the top priority. It may sound tautological, but if you want cheap flights, then prioritize cheap flights. That's it. That's the strategy.

We all say we want cheap flights, but many of us get distracted. We set New Delhi as our goal. We decide we have to take a vacation May 3–10. We prioritize other factors, not realizing that we often do so at the expense of prioritizing cheap flights.

Instead, if cheap flights are the top goal, reverse the standard search process into what I call the Flight First Method:

Step 1: See where the cheapest flights are.
Step 2: Pick one of the cheap flight destinations.
Step 3: Pick one of the cheap flight dates.

To be clear, the Flight First Method doesn't mean only traveling to nearby destinations at unpopular times. As we'll explore in Chapter 7, airfare is not static, and destinations don't have a single, unwavering price. Today's expensive flight may be tomorrow's cheap one.

Let's walk through an example of these two different approaches with our friends Tom and Priya.

After watching *The Sound of Music*, Tom set his heart on going to Austria. He looked up average monthly weather there, and August seemed especially pleasant. With a destination and timeline locked in, he took a look at fares. Cheap flights from the United States to Austria aren't terribly common in general, and especially not in the summer. Unsurprisingly, the cheapest fares Tom found were $1,300 roundtrip. Not a cheap flight by any definition, but Tom had watched fares for a week and they hadn't budged. Fearful that they'd go higher, Tom pulled out his credit card and charged $1,300. He wasn't thrilled to be blowing so much on a single flight, but he figured he had little choice.

"What can you do?" he asked, less a question than a conclusion. The answer is *lots*, but he needed a new strategy from the outset.

Meanwhile, Priya too decided she was itching for a vacation. She didn't set her heart on one particular destination; there were dozens of places she'd be thrilled to visit. And she didn't choose a specific week in advance, preferring to keep her options open instead.

Priya was determined, however, to get a cheap flight, like she had to Hawaii, Guatemala, and Bangkok. Rather than search for flights to only one particular city over one particular week, she instead set about to find where she could fly inexpensively.

First, Priya pulled up Google Flights, set her destination as Europe, and chose the FLEXIBLE DATES option in order to look at one-week trips anytime over the next six months. Perusing the results, she saw that fares happened to be expensive to places like Vienna and Milan, but they were currently under $450 roundtrip to Amsterdam, Barcelona, and Budapest. All three sounded like great places to visit, and after consulting some friends she ultimately decided on Budapest. Because her time off at work was flexible, she let the calendar of cheap flights guide her vacation planning, rather than selecting specific dates in advance. Flights to Budapest happened to be cheap throughout September and October, so she pulled out her credit card and booked a trip to Hungary in early September for $415 roundtrip.

TOM'S AND PRIYA'S SEARCH PROCESSES, COMPARED

Tom (Destination First Method)
Step 1: Picked where he wanted to travel (Vienna)
Step 2: Picked when he wanted to travel (late August)
Step 3: Checked the price
Price paid: $1,300

Priya (Flight First Method)
Step 1: Saw where the cheapest flights were (Amsterdam, Barcelona, and Budapest)
Step 2: Picked one of the cheap flight destinations (Budapest)

Step 3: Picked one of the cheap flight dates (early September)
Price paid: $415

By setting cheap flights as his last concern, Tom paid $1,300 for his European vacation tickets. By putting cheap flights first, Priya paid $415.

In principle, most of us are like Priya, with tons of places we'd be thrilled to go. In practice, most of us are like Tom, kneecapping ourselves from the jump by searching only a narrow set of fares and grudgingly accepting expensive airfare as What It Costs.

Imagine for a moment that all flights are now $250 roundtrip. Where would you go? Greece? Sri Lanka? Zanzibar? Few of us have sat down and listed every place in the world we'd visit if airfare were no concern, but if we did, I suspect most of our lists would number in the hundreds if not thousands. We have countless places we'd visit if flights were cheap, yet so many of us plan a vacation as though there's only one place in the world in which we're interested. Brazil may be at the top of your list, but it's not as though the country will soon disappear and this year is your last chance. Even if cheap Rio flights aren't popping up right now, they will *at some point*, and you'll enjoy Copacabana even more after getting a good deal tomorrow than if you'd overpaid for flights today.

Upending the way you search for flights takes effort. Thinking first of where and when you'd like to travel is certainly a more natural and intuitive approach. But once you've committed to getting cheap flights and made them the top priority, your travel possibilities open up.

Using the Flight First Method didn't just get Priya a cheap

flight to Hungary, it delivered a better vacation as well. By paying $415 for her flight, Priya could use the savings to really splurge in Budapest. She could stay at the Four Seasons hotel with views of the royal castle, sample a caviar-tasting menu at Arany Kaviár, even treat herself to a spa day at one of Budapest's countless thermal baths. With so much money saved on airfare, Priya could afford to indulge during her vacation in a way Tom couldn't.

Plus, as if Tom hadn't been fare-shamed enough, Priya wound up visiting Vienna on that very same trip by using another flight search strategy I'll explain in Chapter 12: building your own layovers.

It wasn't easy for Priya to let go of the Destination First Method of flight searching. Doing so required her to not get too attached to any one destination but instead follow an altogether different approach that she knew would let her travel more: embracing serendipity.

HOW TO EMBRACE SERENDIPITY

Almost every overseas vacation I've taken in the past decade has been a trip I didn't plan to take.

Roundtrip to Milan for $130. Osaka for $169. Barcelona $222. Brussels $225, twice.

I hadn't decided to go to Milan and then searched for flights there. Nor had I actively considered visiting Japan, Spain, or Belgium before buying flights to those very countries. Cheap flights allowed me to see places I didn't even know I'd been missing.

Many cheap flight aficionados have no idea where their next vacation will be. It'd be like asking what's for dinner 134 days from now. This isn't a bug to be fixed but a feature to be celebrated. To do so requires a fundamental shift in the way we think about flights and trip planning, away from a destination-centric approach and toward a cheap-flight–centric one.

I fully appreciate that this mental transformation is neither easy nor intuitive. Nobody daydreams about cheap flights per se. We daydream about eating pastries in a Parisian café or standing up on a surfboard for the first time in Australia. The destination is what inspires us, not the cost of the ride there.

But that doesn't contradict prioritizing cheap flights. On the contrary, putting cheap flights first is the very thing that allows the travel daydreams to come true. Rather than negating one another, they supplement each other. The daydreams fuel the desire to get cheap flights, and the cheap flights give us even more reason to dream.

For instance, I'd never given much thought to visiting the Netherlands until a cheap flight popped up to Amsterdam and my wife and I booked on a whim. We'd heard the Netherlands was a good place for cycling, but it wasn't until we arrived that we realized how remarkable the bike infrastructure throughout the country was. Unlike most countries, rentals were incredibly cheap ($10/day), and even more impressive were the bike lanes. They're everywhere. I live in Portland, Oregon, one of the most cycling-friendly cities in the United States, and our setup is downright laughable compared to the quantity, quality, and safety of bike lanes in the Netherlands. Though we'd always enjoyed leisurely rides, taking them in a place that prioritizes bike infrastructure made us realize how gratifying an activity it can be. Because of that trip, we now place a premium on visiting bike-friendly places, something we never would have discovered about ourselves if we hadn't gotten that fortuitous flight to Amsterdam.

Embracing serendipity in your vacation planning isn't easy; the first step is learning how to handle uncertainty. We crave the satisfaction of having tickets purchased—that's when a trip becomes real, after all—without always recognizing the premium we often pay for that certainty. Many people get stuck booking a $1,000 flight to Europe in the fear that fares will go up rather than holding out for a $400 one. Loss aversion and other cognitive biases can be expensive.

Being serendipitous does not mean booking last minute. That romantic idea of showing up at the airport and picking a destination from the big board is a surefire way of paying ten times more for airfare than your seatmate. Not only are last-minute flights almost always expensive, but as we'll explore in Chapter 11, booking well in advance is superior because it ensures maximal anticipation. Even long-term plans can be serendipitous; my unexpected flights to Osaka and Amsterdam were each booked more than seven months ahead of time.

In fact, the more time you give yourself to book, the easier it will be to welcome uncertainty and serendipity. Priya, who starts monitoring flights six months ahead of travel, has far better odds of finding a cheap flight than Tom, who decided he needs a vacation next month. That's because airfare is volatile, and the exact timing of cheap flights is impossible to predict.

The second component to embracing serendipity is flexibility. If someone asks me whether cheap flights to somewhere in Europe will pop up in the next month, I can give them a categorical yes. If someone asks me whether they'll pop up to Valencia, it's far less certain.

Embracing serendipity is about reshaping your approach. Think of finding airfare as a Russian reversal joke: "In Soviet Russia, cheap flights find you!" Cheap flights are out there, they just need to be prioritized. The earlier you can start your search and the more you can keep your options open, the greater your odds of success.

Another way to think of it is like a bull's-eye.

THE CHEAP FLIGHTS BULL'S-EYE

It was seven o'clock in the morning, the day after Christmas. Who would be calling David this early?

It was his partner, Kristen.

"David. We have to book."

Huh?

"That email list I told you about. They just found flights to Hawaii from Atlanta for under $400."

"Kristen, can this wait? I was asleep."

"No no no, we have to do this right now. It's so cheap. If we wait a few hours and the deal disappears, I will be so upset. We cannot lose Hawaii."

Even a groggy David knew a deal when he heard one. This wasn't the weak tea of saving $40 on flights; this was well over ten times that. He gave his approval—"Merry Christmas!"— Kristen clicked PURCHASE, and soon they were the proud owners of two $377 roundtrip tickets to Hawaii, less than half what they normally go for.

Perhaps even more surprising was the fact that, forty minutes earlier, Kristen hadn't given any thought to a Hawaiian vacation.

"We weren't tracking that by any means, like, 'We've got to go to Hawaii.' We were pretty lax," she told me. "We knew we wanted someplace warm, to get away from the winter blues." Beyond that criterion, though, she was content to sit back and see what good fares popped up.

Kristen did something clever here. If she had set her mind on just one destination, say Bermuda, she might still be waiting for those flights to drop in price. Or if she had been zeroed in on flights to Hawaii but only over her birthday week in May, she never would have noticed $377 flights in March.

Instead, Kristen kept her options open. She was opportunistic. She let cheap flights guide her travel plans, rather than making travel plans first and hoping for cheap flights later. She *optimized* for cheap flights.

In fact, Kristen almost never boxes herself in when it comes to booking vacations. She explained their strategy: "Typically what we do is we'll think, 'Hey, we really want to have a vacation. All right, do we want warm or cold? Are we trying for Europe? Are we trying for the beach?' And then we'll know how many PTO days we're comfortable taking and a general timeframe. We never pick, 'Okay, we're going to fly on this date or that date.' We believe this method has served us well. We typically get the better deals this way."

Think of this approach like an archery range. If you're trying to hit a target the size of a bottle cap, your chances of success are pretty slim. If you're trying to hit a target the size of a tractor, you've got pretty good odds. The more you broaden your preferences, the larger your target, and the better your odds of finding a cheap flight.

Broadening your target doesn't necessarily mean sacrificing. After all, few of us have just one place in the world we want to visit.

Perhaps Aruba is your ideal, but is Hawaii so bad? Put another way, would you pay the normal price of $800 to reach Aruba if you could visit Hawaii for $300? The more we follow Kristen's lead and give ourselves the flexibility to be opportunistic, the more we'll find ourselves awash in cheap flights—and dream vacations.

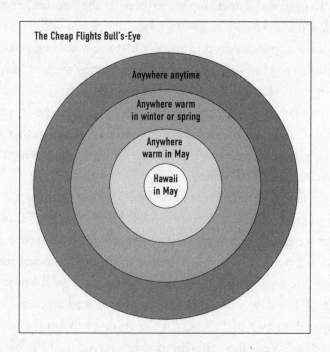

The Cheap Flights Bull's-Eye

Anywhere anytime

Anywhere warm
in winter or spring

Anywhere
warm in May

Hawaii
in May

When that email hit Kristen's inbox the day after Christmas, it was as though the cheap flight overlords were nudging her to visit Hawaii. "Hawaii has always been one of those places, if we get the opportunity, we're going," she said. At $377, she finally had that chance. Remember, Kristen didn't want to book just any flight under $400—ideally it had to be somewhere warm in the next few months. It could just as easily have been Costa Rica or the Galápagos. It just so happened that an employee in the pricing department at American Airlines decided that $377 was what an Atlanta–Honolulu flight should cost that day, and in the process Kristen's vacation fate was sealed.

After their self-professed "spur-of-the-moment booking," Kristen and David wound up enjoying Hawaii even more than they thought they would. They spent a week hiking the Lanikai Pillbox and sailing around Oahu. "It was one of our favorite trips ever," she said. "An absolutely lovely, wonderful, magical place."

David, for his part, has forgiven her for the early-morning wake-up call. It was worth it.

CHEAP FLIGHTS DON'T HAVE
TO BE INCONVENIENT FLIGHTS

When I was twenty-six, I flew the scenic route from Washington, DC, to Denver in order to get the cheapest fare: Baltimore to Newark to Boston to Chicago to Los Angeles to Denver. A nonstop flight would've been about 1,500 miles; my journey was nearly 4,000.

If you think of convenience and price on a grid, most of us hope for tickets in the second box: cheap and convenient. My flight to Denver was way down in the fourth: cheap and highly inconvenient.

The right balance of convenience and price is different for each person, and it changes over your lifetime. In my twenties, I was time rich and cash poor. Why not take a five-stop scented trashbag of a route to Denver if it'll save a few hundred bucks?

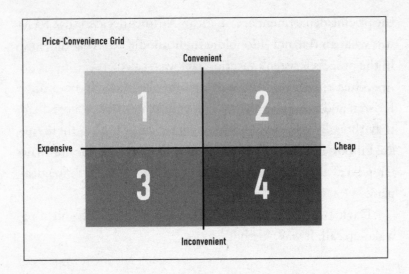

But five-connection itineraries are a young man's game. Now that I've got a family and a young daughter, my priorities have shifted. I'm more inclined to spend discretionary time at home than on a plane. Former *New York Times* travel writer Seth Kugel has a poignant saying: "I'm all for being a miser, but not if it makes you miserable."

The notion that "time is money" can be a helpful mental model for flights. If you want to visit Australia, the most consistently cheap fares require a stop in China en route and 40 hours or more of total travel time. Conversely, it's simple to turn money into time savings: Nonstop flights are almost always more expensive than connecting flights.

Like age, other factors can also change your priorities depending on the trip. If you're traveling with young kids, the quickest itinerary is paramount. If it's a friends' getaway, price may be more important.

Even though it's easy to pay for convenience, there's a widespread misconception I want to dispel: Cheap flights don't have to be inconvenient flights. Anyone who tells you that cheap flights always have horrific fees and multiple connections is doing you a disservice.

Remember that $130 Milan flight that kicked off Scott's Cheap Flights? It was nonstop and included checked baggage. Some cheap flights are roundabout or at weird times, but many aren't. If all you care about is getting the cheapest flight possible, there will be more options at your disposal; if you care about getting cheap *and* convenient flights, there will still be plenty to choose from.

While price is, to me and most people, the most important factor, there are dozens of other factors to be mindful of as well. These include:

- **Time in transit**: The number of stops, length (as well as time of day) of layovers, and total travel time
- **Schedule**: Time of year, day of the week, and time of day
- **Airline quality**: Likelihood of delays or cancellations, ability to rebook if things go awry, how valuable their frequent flyer miles are, and whether you have or are near elite status
- **Airplane quality**: Not just the plane itself (new 787s provide a nicer, smoother ride than old 757s) but also legroom and in-flight amenities, from WiFi to seatback screens to food and drinks to power outlets
- **Fees**: Extra costs if you'll need bags, advance seat selection, or flight changes
- **Airport quality**: Its proximity to you and its propensity for delays or cancellations

- **Fare considerations**: How rare is this fare sale? Can it only be booked on an unheard-of online travel agency, or can it be booked on a major online travel agency (OTA) or directly with the airline? How certain are your travel plans, how far in advance are you booking, and how likely are fares to drop further in the time remaining?

With so many criteria, figuring out what the "best" flight is can feel overwhelming. I have a few pieces of advice.

First, don't let the complexity of finding or comparing flights drag you into nihilism. It can be tempting to throw up your hands when trying to benchmark flight options across dozens of possible factors. But an "lol nothing matters" approach is a sure way to overpay for flights. Again, cheap flights don't happen by accident, they happen when you make them a priority. Though there's always an element of chance—we're at the mercy of how airlines decide to price their tickets—the fact that I've gotten so many cheap flights in my life isn't because I was lucky. It is because I understood and took advantage of strategies that would help me find them.

Second, it's difficult to get the best in every category and still get a cheap fare. Once-a-decade first class mistake fares during peak travel season on the exact route you've been looking for can happen, but they're rare. You're going to have to make trade-offs, even if it's just on one or two factors. Holding out for the perfect cheap flight is a good way to never travel.

Third, you don't have to take into account every one of these factors—or any of them, frankly. If you're the type of person who invariably falls asleep before the plane even takes off, it doesn't make a difference whether there's a seatback screen. If you're 6'6", legroom is paramount. If you're a college student with a thousand dollars in the bank, the only must-have when searching for flights is that they be cheap.

In the end, what you value is a personal decision. There's no right or wrong approach. What's important is having full knowledge of your options and balancing them against your needs. The more must-haves, the fewer options there are, and that's fine. The fewer requirements, though, the larger your bull's-eye and the more cheap flights you'll have to choose from.

Another way to think of it is this: How flexible can you be when planning your next vacation? And what can you do to avoid overpaying for those trips when you don't have any flexibility?

KEY TAKEAWAYS

- Flipping the normal way you search for flights (the Destination First Method) and making price the top priority (the Flight First Method) is the key to finding cheap airfare.

- The fewer must-haves on your list, the larger your cheap flights bull's-eye and the more likely you are to get a good deal.

- Cheap flights don't have to be inconvenient flights. Though each additional criterion means fewer options, bargain hunters still have tons of nonstop routes and summer dates to choose from.

4

FLEXIBILITY:
USING IT TO YOUR ADVANTAGE
(AND WHAT TO DO WHEN YOU DON'T HAVE ANY)

THERE ARE TWO IMPORTANT THINGS TO KNOW ABOUT traveling to Bali.

The first, Shanna Lathwell told me, is that Bali is normally expensive to fly to. Not like we'll-skip-a-few-date-nights expensive. More we-may-as-well-fly-to-Mars expensive.

It had always been a dreamy destination for Shanna's Michigan family. Tropical climate, clear water, world-class snorkeling, and ancient temples. If Detroit had an opposite, it'd be Bali.

Every family divvies up certain responsibilities, and over time Shanna had become the flight guru for hers. Saving money on flights wasn't just something in which she found joy; for her family of five, it was a necessity.

For years, Shanna had kept an eye on flights from Detroit to Bali, but the fares she'd been seeing were north of $2,500 per ticket. "I'd been thinking about it forever," she said, "but flight prices were making it impossible for our family of five to go."

The second thing to know about Bali, though, is that it's pleasantly affordable once you're there. "I knew that if we could get a good price on tickets, the trip once we got there wouldn't be so expensive," Shanna explained.

Dropping $12,500 on economy flights for a family of five is a horror for the cheap flight–loving heart. It was out of the question for the Lathwell family's finances. "Maybe someday when the kids are out of the house," Shanna reflected.

Dejected though she was, Shanna kept an eye on Bali fares because, hey, daydreams are free. Sure enough, when a Scott's Cheap Flights deal alert hit her inbox in April 2018, she saw her opportunity.

Though flights out of Detroit would have meant thousands of dollars out of pocket (not to mention two or three connections for somewhere as far-flung as Bali), the email alerted Shanna to flights from Chicago to Bali for just $550 roundtrip, with a single connection and on a five-star airline. Reluctant to get her hopes up, Shanna checked fares on Google Flights for dates around her kids' spring break, expecting to see the four-figure prices she was used to seeing.

Instead, when $550 ticket prices popped up on her screen, she couldn't believe it. "I was shocked," she said.

Shanna did some quick mental math. She could buy flights for her entire family from Chicago to Bali for roughly the price of just a single ticket from Detroit. The prospect of saving $10,000 on flights—not to mention visiting a beautiful and remote bucket-list destination—convinced Shanna, who soon announced the news to her family: They'd all be spending spring break in Bali.

What can we learn from Shanna's example? A few lessons:

Keep an eye on driving-distance airports: Flights out of Chicago aren't restricted to residents of Chicago, like a locals-only pass at the village swimming pool. Yes, O'Hare International Airport is easier to access for residents of Chicago than those of Detroit, but with modern vehicles and highways, even out-of-staters can take advantage. Don't get myopic and only ever consider your nearest airport.

I don't mean to be flip, but it's easy to overlook nearby but not immediate airports. When I got that $130 nonstop roundtrip flight from New York City to Milan, I was living in Washington, DC. If I'd only considered flights out of DC, I'd have paid $850 (or, more accurately, I wouldn't have gone to Milan). By expanding my search to include NYC—with full knowledge that I could take a $20 bus up from DC and even go a day or two early to visit friends—I saved $700 on my trip.

Was taking the bus to NYC worth $700 to me? No question. Was driving to Chicago worth $10,000 to Shanna? Of course. It's not that flights out of Detroit wouldn't have been more convenient. It's that they weren't *$10,000* more convenient. Think back to the price-convenience grid in the previous chapter: Though the ideal is always convenient and cheap (the second box), some tickets—like mine to Milan and Shanna's to Bali—are worth edging into cheap and inconvenient.

Driving to a nearby airport means paying for parking, but there are plenty of ways to avoid getting gouged. Though airport parking is usually expensive, most facilities have reasonably priced long-term economy lots if you'll be gone more than a week. Or you could do what Shanna did and book a Park/Sleep/Fly package: a one-night stay at a nearby hotel (usable on either end of the trip), a shuttle to the airport, and free parking for the duration of the trip. When they landed back in Chicago at nine o'clock at night, rather than having to drive straight to Detroit after a long flight and getting in past midnight, they used their hotel night, got some rest, and drove home in the morning.

Keep an eye on short-hop airports: Searching nearby airports isn't just restricted to those within driving distance. My friend Matt in Kansas City recently told me about scooping up $271 roundtrip tickets on Delta from Dallas to Barcelona. It would have been an exceptionally long drive to get to Dallas, so instead, he booked a Southwest flight to Dallas for $98 roundtrip, bringing his total cost for a flight to Spain to $369. Out of curiosity, he searched for flights from Kansas City to Spain that same day: $1,330.

In a perfect world, flight search engines would let Matt buy a single itinerary composed of the $98 Southwest flight and the $271 Delta flight. In reality, as we'll explore in Chapter 8, airlines won't sell one another's flights unless they have a partnership. Southwest doesn't offer flights to Europe at all, and Delta was charging over $1,300 to fly him from Kansas City to Barcelona.

Instead, when an amazing deal pops up only from a nearby airport, cheap flight aficionados do the extra work themselves. First, they book the long-haul flight, and after that they figure out the best way to reach the jump-off airport. (By the way, these two flights don't need to be booked simultaneously; Matt didn't book his Southwest flight until a month after booking Dallas–Barcelona.)

What's more, Matt scheduled his flights to leave a buffer day in the middle, for two reasons. First, doing so minimized the risk that a delay on his flight to Dallas would cause him to miss the flight to Barcelona. Second, that buffer day let him spend time exploring Dallas with his buddy living there, a free stopover strategy we'll discuss at greater length in Chapter 12.

Think about total travel time, not flight time: Thinking holistically about travel time can be a helpful exercise, and that's precisely what Shanna did. Most itineraries from Detroit to Bali consist of at least two stops and 35 hours of total travel time. Shanna's flight from Chicago to Bali had one stop and a total travel time of about 25 hours. Add on the five hours it took to drive from Detroit to Chicago and she wound up with a 30-hour trip. If Shanna's family were racing their neighbors who were flying out of Detroit, the Lathwells would have had enough time for lunch, drinks, a surfing lesson, and a massage by the time their neighbors landed in Bali.

Patience: Shanna had kept an eye on flights to Bali for years. Though $2,500 flights were out of the question, she didn't bite when those fares jostled around at the margin. Even a 20 percent drop, after all, still meant $2,000 a ticket and $10,000 for the family. She didn't just wait for fares to be good in a relative sense; she waited until they were good in an absolute sense. Recognizing that Detroit–Bali flights were unlikely to ever drop below $1,000, she bided her time and was opportunistic when the $550 Chicago fares appeared.

Being flexible about where you fly from only makes sense when the savings outweigh the inconvenience. If Shanna's family had saved only $20 per ticket for flights out of Chicago, they would've spent that on gas money alone.

There's no objective threshold where price offsets convenience because each person values their money and time differently—and those preferences can change by age and circumstance. When I was twenty-three years old, I would've happily taken a six-hour bus ride if it saved me $30. At thirty-three, I'd prefer those six hours. Even today, if I'm traveling alone I optimize for price, but if I'm traveling with my infant daughter, convenience is paramount.

Regardless of whether you're optimizing for money or convenience, it's important to recognize that nearby airports give you flexibility. There's nothing wrong with prioritizing convenience over money, but it's best to do so *consciously* because you preferred a specific more expensive flight, rather than *unconsciously* because you weren't aware of other options at your disposal.

What does this look like in practice? If you have a specific trip in mind, the first step in most people's search is putting in their ideal route and dates and seeing what fares come up. The key is to not *end* your search there. If Shanna had only ever looked at flights from Detroit, she'd still be wondering to this day if her family would ever make it to Bali. By expanding her scope—and taking advantage of Google Flights' ability to search up to seven cities at once (discussed at greater length in Chapter 8)—she was able to get an even better itinerary at a fifth of the price.

Though Shanna didn't have total flexibility—the goal was a family trip to Bali, not just anywhere—she shrewdly resisted booking too early and overpaying for flights. Where others might have simply accepted expensive airfare as the price of admission, Shanna was both patient in waiting for fares to drop and wise to pull the trigger quickly when they did, rather than vacillating on the decision.

But how do you know when is the right—and, as important, the wrong—time to book flights? It's one of the most vexing dilemmas in travel planning. Time it well and you could be the gleeful owner of a certified cheap flight. Time it poorly and you could be out hundreds or more.

Most airlines (with a few notable exceptions, like Southwest) begin selling flights a year out from travel. If you want to take a flight on June 17, 2022, the absolute earliest you'd be able to book that flight would be June 17, 2021. And unless it gets sold out, you can theoretically book a flight up until a few minutes before takeoff.

Fares will swing wildly during the twelve months you could book a given flight. With so much pressure to book at the right time, how do you know when that is?

BEWARE BAD ADVICE

Chances are you've heard a lot of different advice about the best time to book flights.

In a quest for clicks, some companies try to take advantage of the confusion and opacity around flight pricing by claiming they have unlocked the hidden "best time" to book. Each claims to have conducted the most scientifically sound study, and yet their conclusions are all over the map, from Tuesday at 3 p.m. (FareCompare) to Sunday at 5 a.m. (Skyscanner) to anytime on a Thursday (Hopper) to anytime on a Sunday (Expedia) to simply August 23 (CheapOair).

All of these analyses are misleading because they rely on a fundamentally flawed metric: average ticket prices.

Studies claiming to have uncovered a fixed best time to book flights are all structured in the same way: They take a large dataset of airfares, find the average ticket price of all those fares for each day of the week, and then declare one day (or specific time) superior to the rest.

The problem is that they're all answering the wrong question. If the question were about long-term trends in airfare, average ticket price would be useful data. But the question they're claiming to answer is when should you book a flight in order to get the cheapest fare. On this matter, average ticket price tells you almost nothing.

To understand why, consider this simplified example. Say on September 1 you search for Christmas fares from Los Angeles to Rome. Half of the fares come back priced at $500 and the other half are priced at $700, giving an average price of $600. You search the same tickets again a month later, on October 1. This time, half the fares are priced at $300, and half are priced at $1,000, giving an average ticket price of $650.

If you're looking at the average ticket price, September's $600 average beats October's $650—but if you're just trying to get a cheap flight, October is the clear winner. After all, you can't actually book average fares; you can only book available fares.

Using average ticket price as a road map for booking cheap flights is as sensible as a college student getting into an elevator with Warren Buffett and celebrating his newfound status as a billionaire. On average, it's true; in reality, it's nonsense.

The fundamental problem with retrospective studies is

that they don't have any predictive power. They're building a model that overfits historical data too closely, rather than a model designed to forecast the future. You may as well look at last year's stock market returns, find the day with the highest performance, and declare that that's the best day to buy stocks every year.

Instead of following the charlatan advice of The Averagers, what's important to remember is that the best time to book is when cheap flights pop up. Though "book flights when they're cheap" may sound reductive, I stress this mundane point because it's essential to keep the focus on monitoring for cheap flights rather than preselecting an arbitrary date or time to book.

It's impossible to say *precisely* when a specific deal will pop up. The best deals Scott's Cheap Flights found in 2019—$98 roundtrip to Hawaii on March 4, $280 roundtrip to China on June 27, $177 roundtrip to Barcelona on December 4—came with no advance notice. Nothing from 2018's deals could have told us that March 4, June 27, and December 4 would be great days for cheap flights the following year.

Even without exact certainty, though, we can still have a broad sense of when to expect cheap flights. Think of the weather in Seattle. Will it rain on October 26? Hard to say. But will it be generally rainy this autumn? Almost certainly. So it is with projecting airfare. Although there's no static calendar date for when fares are cheapest, there is a framework for when cheap flights are most likely to pop up. I call these Goldilocks Windows.

GOLDILOCKS WINDOWS FOR DOMESTIC
AND INTERNATIONAL TRIPS

The first thing to keep in mind is that airfare pricing is incredibly complex nowadays. As we'll explore in Chapter 7, flight prices, largely controlled by convoluted algorithms, can swing by the hour, if not by the minute. Airfare isn't static or stable, it's highly volatile.

Second, airlines have a set number of seats they're trying to sell on a given flight. They want to get as much money as possible for those seats, of course, but they face a few unique difficulties:

1. **Rival goods**: If I buy a seat, that seat can't be sold to someone else.
2. **Spoilage**: Seats have an expiration date (at takeoff).
3. **Unpredictability**: When (or if) travelers will book a seat is highly uncertain.

These factors make pricing decisions difficult for airlines. If eleven months before takeoff they sell a bunch of $300 seats to Paris, the airline can't later sell those seats to others willing to pay more. The price is locked in because airplane seats are rival goods. That's why when flights first become available—the earliest any airline starts selling flights is a year out from departure—they're rarely cheap. At the same time, if the airline keeps fares higher than what most travelers will pay, they risk spoilage: flying with too many empty seats. Airlines create complex models trying to predict exactly when travelers will book and how much they'd be willing to pay, but there's always an intrinsic amount of uncertainty.

Though you've probably heard advice to book flights early, keep in mind it's not the *earliest* bird that gets the worm. Fares don't linearly increase from Day 1 to Day 365; they constantly zig and zag. Unless you stumble upon a truly exceptional fare, it's generally a bad idea to book flights too early. That's because if fares later drop, few airlines will refund you the difference.

Like early-bird fares, last-minute fares tend to be inflated as well. More on this in Chapter 7, but in short, the price of flights tends to skyrocket in the last few weeks before departure, and especially in the last few days, as airlines try to maximize revenue from late-booking business travelers. The Hall of Cheap Flight Shame is filled with travelers who thought they might score a better deal by waiting to book until the last minute.

Rather than aiming to book flights just as they become available or waiting until a week before departure, I recommend following the Goldilocks Principle: Don't book too early or too late. Aim for somewhere right in the middle.

The sweet spot will vary depending on when and where you're traveling. In general, international flights are most likely to go on sale two to eight months ahead of time, while domestic flights are most likely to drop one to three months before travel. If you're looking to travel during a peak time—summer, Christmas, a major local holiday like St. Patrick's Day in Ireland—add a few months extra to those recommendations.

GOLDILOCKS WINDOWS FOR CHEAP FLIGHTS		
SEASON	DOMESTIC	INTERNATIONAL
Off-peak	1 to 3 months before travel	2 to 8 months before travel
Peak	3 to 7 months before travel	4 to 10 months before travel

There's an old saying in aviation: "Altitude is your friend." If there's a problem with the plane, you'd rather be 30,000 feet above the ground than 300 feet up. The very same principle applies to searching for flights. The earlier in those ranges you start monitoring, the better chance you'll have of coming across a cheap flight. You're far more likely to find one if you've given yourself eight months rather than eight days.

To be clear, you don't want to book just *any* fare during these recommended periods, only a great one. At the same time, when you do see an outstanding fare, book it! Resist the temptation to mull it over for a while, thinking it'll definitely stick around. There's a Hotcakes Principle to booking flights: The better a fare, the shorter it will last. If you found a great fare but you're not 100 percent sure about booking, use the 24-hour rule (detailed in Chapter 12) to lock in the price and give yourself a day to decide.

EXAMPLES OF GREAT ROUNDTRIP FARES OUT OF MAJOR U.S. CITIES, CIRCA 2019 (VARIES SOMEWHAT ON SPECIFIC ROUTE)

- Canada: $200
- Transcontinental United States: $250
- Mexico: $250
- Central America: $300
- Western Europe: $400
- Hawaii/Alaska: $400
- Northern South America: $450
- China: $400
- Eastern Europe: $500
- Southeast Asia: $550
- Japan/Korea: $600
- South Asia: $650
- Africa: $700
- Australia/New Zealand: $700
- Southern South America: $700
- Middle East: $700
- Central Asia: $700
- South Pacific: $750

With any trip, a mix of skill, timing, and luck are critical to getting the cheapest fares. Skill is needed to know *not* to book when fares are currently high but have a good chance of dropping. Timing is essential in order to act quickly—the Hotcakes Principle—when fares drop abnormally low. And finally, unless you happen to be an airline revenue manager, remember that there's always an element of luck because ticket prices are outside our control. Although we can have a good sense of trends, history, and odds, there's never a guarantee any given route will drop in price.

But what if you've been monitoring and no cheap flights appeared during the period when they were most likely to pop up? Assuming it's a trip you have to take and there's little flexibility (like a friend's wedding, say), at a certain point, the goal switches from getting a cheap flight to not getting hosed. You may have been holding out for $200 roundtrip flights to New Orleans, but once it gets to four or six weeks before travel, at that point I'd recalibrate my expectations and hope to get away with paying $350, rather than waiting until the last minute and paying $600.

SET YOURSELF A 21-DAY CALENDAR REMINDER

I recently had to book a flight to Atlanta, and because of schedule constraints there was one specific Delta flight I needed. The fare was decent but not great when I started monitoring about six weeks out from travel. I checked the flight daily, hoping that the price would come down. But rather than continuing to monitor up until the last day, I set myself a calendar reminder to book exactly three weeks ahead of travel.

Why did I set that specific day as my deadline? Because the cheapest tickets regularly include a 21-day advance purchase requirement in their fare rules. Even though the ticket I was monitoring hadn't gotten cheaper in the preceding few weeks like I'd hoped it would, I booked it because I knew that the cheapest fares would expire after Day 21.

Lo and behold, the day after I booked, the fare shot up by $140, and then a week later another $150 as the next cheapest fare's 14-day advance purchase requirement passed. Setting myself a 21-day deadline (and a calendar reminder to make sure I wouldn't forget) prevented me from accidentally overpaying.

Though there's no definitive cheapest time of year to *book* flights, there are unquestionably cheaper (and more expensive) times to fly.

THE CHEAPEST TIMES TO TRAVEL

In general, Tuesday, Wednesday, and Saturday are the cheapest days to travel. Friday, Sunday, and Monday are usually the most expensive days. Why? Airlines trying to gouge business travelers. As we'll go over in Chapter 7, businesspeople generally prefer to fly out on Sundays or Mondays and return home on Fridays. They rarely travel in the middle of the week or the middle of the weekend, so airlines price those fares lower to appeal to leisure travelers.

Seasonally, the fall and winter months tend to be cheapest, with the major exception of mid-December through early January. With schools and many businesses closed, the Christmas/New Year's period is one of the most popular (and therefore expensive) times of the year to travel. Spring often has good deals, though as the calendar progresses into late May and especially June, the availability of cheap flights quickly diminishes.

By far the most difficult three months of the year to get cheap flights are (in ascending order of difficulty): June, August, and July. Summer is the most popular time of year to travel, for two primary reasons: great weather and school's on break. Humans are fond of sunshine and warmth; many of us are inclined to get out when it's nice out. For millions of students, teachers, and parents, though, summer is the only time of year that it's even possible to take a vacation. This surge in travelers causes a surge in fares.

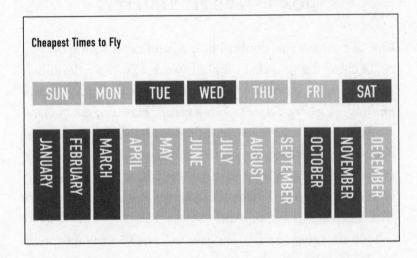

Cheapest Times to Fly

| SUN | MON | TUE | WED | THU | FRI | SAT |

JANUARY · FEBRUARY · MARCH · APRIL · MAY · JUNE · JULY · AUGUST · SEPTEMBER · OCTOBER · NOVEMBER · DECEMBER

If nice weather is your primary motivation for summer travel, there's a simple way to do it cheaper: Take advantage of Southern Hemisphere geographic arbitrage. January through March is one of the cheapest times of year to fly internationally departing the Northern Hemisphere, precisely when it's summertime in places like Argentina, Australia, and South Africa.

But if you're a student, teacher, parent, or just someone

whose ability to travel is restricted to June through August, you're stuck competing against millions of other travelers for the most popular seats. Apart from scouting out cheap summer flights many months in advance, the other way to get a good deal is to travel as early or late in the summer as possible. Flights in early June or late August are significantly more likely to be cheap (or at least not egregiously expensive) than flights in July.

WHAT ABOUT WHEN YOU DON'T HAVE FLEXIBILITY?

One of the recurring doubts I hear when I'm preaching the gospel of cheap flights is that they only work if you have flexibility.

Scott, what if I can't be serendipitous? Cheap flights are great and all, but what if I need to fly to a specific place on a specific date?

It's true that the more flexibility you have, the greater your odds of getting a cheap flight. If you live in Chicago and want to visit anywhere in Europe anytime this fall, as long as you start looking at least 3 or 4 months in advance, it's a virtual certainty that cheap flights will pop up.

On the other hand, if you have to be in Vienna on September 22 for your sister's destination wedding, the chances of a cheap flight popping up from Chicago to Austria around that specific timeframe are considerably lower.

Before we get into strategies you can use to get the best possible deal when you don't have flexibility, it's worth first considering when you're truly in a pickle and when you may have more flexibility at your disposal than you realize.

With some trips, your destination and dates are pretty well

locked in. When you're traveling for a wedding or a reunion or to be home for the holidays, you don't have a ton of leeway. You've got a smaller Cheap Flights Bull's-Eye.

Sometimes you have flexibility about *when* you go, even if where you go is set in stone. If you're flying home to visit family or you're in a long-distance relationship and looking for a time to visit, the destination may be set but you have tons of flexibility about when to fly. On the flip side, perhaps you're planning a honeymoon right after the wedding. Your dates are fairly locked in, but you and your partner have tons of flexibility about where you go.

SHOULD I GET TRAVEL INSURANCE?

Some people think I'm reckless for never buying travel insurance, but I've got a good reason: My credit card's already got me covered. Many credit cards automatically carry travel protections at no cost, as long as you use the card to pay for your flight. The specifics will vary by card, but they often include compensation for flight delays or cancellations (including reimbursement for lodging and meals, if necessary), lost, damaged, or delayed bags, rental car insurance, sometimes even foreign medical insurance. (If, like me, you find it hard to memorize your card's specifics, just Google [the name of your credit card] + travel protections.)

Because my credit card already carries travel insurance, buying additional insurance would often be superfluous. This is especially true considering that, contrary to popular perception, travel insurance (whether you paid for it or it was included on your credit card) doesn't let you cancel a flight penalty-free. For that, you have to book a much more expensive ticket to begin with.

Where many people accidentally paint themselves into a corner is by voluntarily forfeiting flexibility on normal vacations. As we explored in Chapter 3, most people use a Destination First Method, choosing where and when they want to travel before looking at fares. Flipping that approach and employing the Flight First Method is the best way to avoid overpaying for flights, but it also means putting less priority on one specific destination or one specific set of dates. Giving yourself flexibility on where and when you fly is the single most important way to find a cheap flight, and yet we commonly surrender it from the outset because that's how we're used to planning trips.

I stress this point not to be a nag who says you should only ever fly wherever is cheapest. You're allowed to have preferences, of course. I'm just encouraging you to put airfare in context. Few of us would go to a restaurant, reject the waiter's offer to look at the menu, and order the rib eye with zero consideration for price or other options. But that's exactly what many of us do with flights. We set our heart on one specific vacation, price be damned. If Prague is at the top of your list, would you still pay $1,000 for flights if you knew there were $250 flights to Paris? Knowing what else is available gives you a real choice on how much you value going to City A over City B.

SOUTHWEST AIRBITRAGE

The minute I get a wedding invitation (or similarly inflexible event), I'll book myself a flight on Southwest. Unlike most airlines, Southwest doesn't charge fees to cancel a ticket. So by booking through them, I've locked in the price and ensured that's the maximum price I'll have to pay. If I decide not to go, I can cancel the ticket for free. If prices drop on Southwest or a better or cheaper flight pops up on another airline, I can cancel and rebook. And if nothing better pops up, I'll know I got the best deal I could.

With those caveats said, let's say you need to fly somewhere, and you truly have to be there on a specific date. What then? That was the situation Patrick Kane unexpectedly found himself in recently.

When his partner's elderly father fell ill, Patrick began figuring out how to fly the family to Dominica to see him. He looked up flights but was disheartened to find airfare from Fort Lauderdale to Dominica was almost $700 per person. Instead of paying $2,000 total for himself, his partner, and her son, Patrick got an alert about a cheap flight from Fort Lauderdale to Martinique for $138 roundtrip. "After landing in Martinique, we took the ferry to Dominica," Patrick wrote. "We had a wonderful time with her father. Plus, we enjoyed Martinique."

Though he didn't have flexibility about when (as soon as possible) or where (Dominica) they traveled, Patrick was clever in his approach. Rather than searching only for flights to Dominica, he checked nearby airports as well. Though it required the time and expense of a ferry ride, the flight to Martinique was over $500 per person cheaper than one to Dominica. A no-brainer.

It's not just destination airports; if you're trying to get a good deal and don't have much flexibility, do like Shanna did on her Bali vacation and check out nearby departure airports as well. I recently saw flights from Atlanta to Madrid for $235 roundtrip. If you lived in Knoxville and needed to get to Spain, rather than paying $1,300 for flights out of Tennessee, you could book the $235 flight from Atlanta and make the three-hour drive. Or if you don't like driving, you could hop a $130 roundtrip flight from Knoxville to Atlanta, bringing your total cost to $365.

Another tactic is to tinker a bit with the travel dates. Sometimes altering by a day or two on either side can save hundreds in airfare. For example, my friend George was once flying from DC to Las Vegas for a bachelor party, and airfare was hovering around $480 roundtrip—higher than it should've been. He'd initially planned to depart on Thursday afternoon and take a red-eye back on Sunday evening. I suggested he check what fares would be if he returned on Monday instead of Sunday. He was reluctant because he had an important work meeting Monday afternoon, but we did a quick search just to see. The original flight was scheduled to depart Sunday at 11:50 p.m., but it turned out that if he changed the date to Monday, there was a flight leaving at 12:50 a.m.—just an hour later—that brought the total fare down to $260. Though he went on to lose that $220 savings playing craps, he said it was still a moral victory.

What if you don't have somewhere specific you need to be, but you do have a rigid time-off schedule? Alice Murray recently found herself in this situation, eager to take her mom on a trip but having to work around the academic calendar. She knew her mom had a week off in February, so rather than decide beforehand where they would go, Alice let serendipity guide them. When a $390 roundtrip flight from Boston to Barcelona popped up in her inbox, including availability over the very week she needed, she called her mom right away. "Instead of tears and an immediate need for life advice, I had a mother-daughter trip proposition that she couldn't say no to," Alice wrote. "She agreed to travel 'my style' by going for a cheap flight deal and figuring out the details later." Though they had little flexibility about when to travel, by giving themselves flexibility about *where* to travel, they bettered their odds and wound up with a cheap flight to Spain.

Let's say none of these tips work for your situation. You know the exact flight and the exact dates you need. Even with little wiggle room, you've still got an arrow left in your quiver that we discussed earlier this chapter: when to book.

Imagine you live in Los Angeles and your sister just announced her bachelorette party will be in Nashville the following May, eight months from now. You can't take more than a few days off work, so you'll need a flight that leaves after work on Thursday, gets you into Nashville as early as possible on Friday, and returns the following Tuesday evening. You've got no flexibility about where you go, nor can you show up late or dip out early; it's your sister's bachelorette party. The only flight that fits all those criteria is a nonstop on American, but when you check, roundtrip fares are $550.

You could theoretically book right now, but $550 for that route is very much on the high end. Or you could wait and monitor that flight, either by setting yourself a calendar reminder to check daily or by setting up an alert tracker through Google Flights or Kayak. Remember, the window when cheap domestic flights are most likely to pop up is typically one to three months in advance of travel. They can pop up earlier, but it's less common.

Though actually booking your Nashville flight eight months ahead of time would be bad if fares are $550, it's prudent to start monitoring as soon as you know your plans. This is doubly true when searching for routes or dates where cheap flights are rare, like deals to India or peak summer flights. By starting to keep an eye on fares eight months ahead of time, you have far more runway for a cheap fare to pop up than if you'd started searching just a month in advance.

The key—and admittedly difficult!—question to ask yourself is whether a fare you're seeing is more likely to go up or down in the time you have left to book. When you search Los Angeles–Nashville, Google Flights estimates the typical fare is between $225 to $530 roundtrip. While I'd caution against using Google's exact numbers—paying $520 roundtrip from Los Angeles to Nashville is terrible, not typical—it's helpful to get a ballpark sense of what's normal. If you've got eight months before your trip and fares are $550, no question you should hold out for fares closer to $250 or even $200. If you've got one month left and flights are $300, at that point you have little runway left and it's better to book the not-great-not-terrible fare, lest you get stuck with an exorbitant last-minute fare.

Every person has a different tolerance for risk. Some people would rather lock in a $300 flight early and avoid stressing themselves out, while others prefer to patiently wait for a fare they'd consider truly cheap: $225 or less. Either way, the more lead time you can give yourself to monitor, the better your odds of getting a cheap flight.

FLEXIBILITY IS A CURRENCY

I've devoted an entire chapter to flexibility for a simple reason: It's the single most important factor in boosting your cheap flight odds.

Focusing solely on one destination is like playing Whac-A-Mole but keeping your attention laser-focused on one hole, hoping the rodent pops up there. Cheap flights are popping up all around, meanwhile, and you're missing them. A $250 roundtrip flight to Geneva pops up, but it was out of sight because you were looking only at flights to Germany. A $400 roundtrip flight to Bangkok goes on sale for April, but you missed it because you only considered flights to Thailand in May.

The more criteria you put forth, the fewer cheap flights will suffice. That's true not just across where and when you go, but other constraints as well. Are you willing only to fly your favorite airline, or will you go with the cheapest fare if it's on a different carrier? Will you take only nonstop flights, or would you take a connecting flight if it's $300 cheaper?

There are dozens of variables one could consider essential or flexible when looking at flights, but for most people it boils down to three primary factors:

- Where to fly?
- When to go?
- When to book?

If it feels intimidating to optimize for cheap flights by having no prerequisites at all, try choosing one of these three considerations and centering your trip on that.

Pick Portugal. The next good deal to Lisbon that drops, grab it—without deciding in advance when to travel or when to book. And if nothing good is popping up, perhaps you broaden your scope a bit. Book the next cheap flight from New York to Lisbon (paired with a flight from your home airport to New York), or the next cheap flight to Madrid (paired with an onward flight to Lisbon).

Or pick the spring. It's a slow season at work and you shouldn't have any problem getting time off. When a good deal pops up with availability from April through June, that's your ticket. You're not deciding in advance where you'll go or precisely when you'll book because you know cheap flights are impossible to predict on a granular level.

Or pick the next good deal. You recently broke up with your significant other and could use something fun to look forward to. You and your best friend decide that the next cheap flight out of your home airport, you're going to book it. Where and when you'll go is up to the cheap flight overlords, and that's fine. The goal, after all, is to get your mind off the breakup and on to the excitement of an upcoming trip.

You're allowed to have nonnegotiables, of course. Perhaps New Zealand is your mother's dream destination and you want to treat her to a retirement trip. Or you have young kids and can travel only during a school break. While the Flight First Method works great for most vacations, it isn't practicable for every trip we take. Sometimes factors other than price need to take precedence.

Consider any potential requisites carefully, though. There's no free lunch; each additional need-to-have narrows the likelihood of cheap flights popping up. If cheap flights are a goal, flexibility is a valuable currency that ought to be used wisely.

KEY TAKEAWAYS

- Keeping an eye on nearby airports—including ones within driving distance and even a short-hop flight—can vastly increase your odds of getting a cheap flight. In many instances, using a nearby airport can also mean less overall travel time.
- Though there's no specific cheapest time to book flights, fares are most likely to become cheap two to eight months in advance for international travel and one to three months in advance for domestic travel.
- The cheapest times of year to travel are fall and winter, and the cheapest days of the week are Tuesday, Wednesday, and Saturday. Summers, peak holidays, Mondays, and Fridays tend to be the most expensive.
- The more flexibility you can give yourself, the better your odds of getting a cheap flight. When you have little flexibility, your best hope is to book well in advance, when fares are more likely to be low.

5

THEN AND NOW:
A BRIEF HISTORY OF HOW
AIRLINES DETERMINE PRICES

ONE QUESTION I CONSTANTLY GET ASKED IS: "HOW CAN airlines afford to sell $300 roundtrip flights to Europe?"

It's a reasonable question. After all, you sit in a metal tube hurtling through the sky at near supersonic speeds, spending that nine-hour trip wondering "How much longer?" as you flip to the next movie on your seatback screen, and soon land safely on another continent—and a flight home as well—all for less than an average monthly car payment. It feels preposterous—especially in light of the fact that, not too long ago, it was quite rare to fly to Europe for under $1,000 roundtrip.

My answer usually elicits some measure of disbelief: It's true that airlines are making little profit on your $300 economy ticket to Germany, but the reason why is that they don't need to. Nowadays, airlines make their money elsewhere.

To understand how an industry can afford to fly you to Europe and back for $300 and still make tens of billions of dollars per year, it's helpful to first look back at how airlines used to make money and the ways in which that's evolved over the years. Once we have a fuller sense of how the industry operates, we can use that knowledge to grasp the seemingly incomprehensible behavior of airfare.

1920S–1940S: AIRMAIL AND THE ADVENT OF PASSENGER FLIGHTS

Initially, passengers weren't the focus of air travel; mail was. In the early 1920s, the U.S. Post Office was, in effect, the largest airline in the world. Flying was expensive and dangerous at the time, though, and the federal government began to privatize airmail with the Kelly Act in 1925. Dozens of private airlines were created over the next decade to compete for these mail contracts, including what would become three of the largest U.S. airlines today, Delta, American, and United.

Early on, airlines were paid by the government according to the weight of mail they carried, but postage was charged by the piece. This created a perverse arbitrage opportunity, as Tim Brady detailed in *The American Aviation Experience*:

> It did not take a rocket scientist to figure out that on the weight-mileage formula, the airlines could make money by sending mail to themselves. For example, at 5 cents per ounce, a pound of mail or freight would cost 80 cents to ship 1,000 miles or less. The carrier was paid up to $3 for

this. Therefore, a carrier could send its own mail by air to itself and pocket $2.20 per pound, less operating costs. It was not long before the airmail carriers were mailing themselves bricks, aircraft engines, and heavy telephone books.

So while flying mail was quite profitable for airlines, carrying passengers wasn't. Unlike passengers, mail doesn't care about a comfortable seat or a reasonable cabin temperature or arriving on time. Brady estimated that by the late 1920s mail was six times more profitable to carry than passengers. Though some airlines did sell seats to the public on airmail routes, no airline at the time catered exclusively to passengers.

To incoming president Herbert Hoover, who dreamed of a future for passenger planes, this was a major problem. With the goal of fostering an airline industry that primarily flew people instead of things, he signed into law the Airmail Act of 1930, which changed the reimbursement formula to discourage mailing bricks and encourage airlines to develop larger planes and carry more passengers.

Though the effort was initially marred by a corruption scandal over which airlines received which contracts, the goal of boosting commercial aviation was a major success. Airlines went from selling six thousand passenger tickets in 1930 to over a million in 1938, diversifying their income away from postal contracts. However, it wasn't until after World War II that commercial air travel became truly widespread.

1950S–1970S: FLIGHTS AS A LUXURY GOOD AND THE BEGINNING OF AIR TOURISM

With the nation awash in planes left over from the war, and with the advent of new passenger-friendly technology like pressurized cabins and onboard toilets, America was entering what we look back on as the "golden age" of flying. It was becoming a more mainstream way to travel.

At the time, commercial airlines were heavily regulated by the Civil Aeronautics Board, which since 1938 controlled which airlines could fly, what routes they could offer, and how much they could charge passengers.* The CAB's chief concern wasn't making airfare affordable; it was nurturing the nascent airline industry and preventing "destructive, oppressive, or wasteful competition." That may seem silly or antiquated to modern ears, but the CAB had good reason to take a protectionist approach, as one CAB member, Harold Jones, detailed:

> During the early years of the Civil Aeronautics Act it was generally agreed by the operators that special personal services such as stewardesses, free meals, advance reservations, extra-comfortable seats, and limousine service to and from airports were necessary to help overcome the reluctance of the general public to fly.

---

* It was initially known as the Civil Aeronautics Authority before merging with the Air Safety Board in 1940 to become the Civil Aeronautics Board.

Given the expense and novelty, just being able to fly was a luxury. Originally there was no first class per se; *everything* was first class, and every passenger paid the same price. But in 1948, as postwar America hungered for more plane travel, one carrier proposed an innovative business model that would become the basis of how airlines sold tickets for the next seventy years and counting: price discrimination. (The term "discrimination" is used not pejoratively in this case but to illustrate the airlines' pursuit of a maximum willingness to pay from each traveler rather than selling one-size-fits-all tickets.)

Capital Airlines, struggling to turn a profit using the CAB's standard airfare rate, proposed creating a new class of service on its New York–Chicago flights, "air coach." Rather than flying 40-seat planes and charging 6 cents per passenger-mile, Capital asked for permission to put 60 seats on its planes and charge passengers 4 cents per mile. The CAB gave its blessing to the 33 percent fare reduction under a few conditions, including:

- High-density seating arrangements had to be used.
- Flights had to be scheduled at off-hours.
- Costs had to be minimized, including cutting meals and extra flight attendants.

It was a historic move. In a shift toward the modern aviation industry we've come to know, this was the first time that the CAB allowed passengers to have a choice among classes of service: higher fares for first class at convenient times; lower fares for coach at inconvenient times. The concept of cheap flights was born.

Because nothing in life is free, the advent of cheap fares came with some less celebrated changes. Denser seat layouts, inconvenient flight times, no meals, fewer attendants, connecting rather than nonstop flights. But passengers showed they were willing to sacrifice comfort to save money, and within a year, almost every major airline had adopted the air coach model. By 1952, cheaper transatlantic "tourist class" flights had begun.

(As an aside, it's important to remember that even the cheapest overseas coach flights at the time cost nearly $5,000 roundtrip in 2019 dollars, and thus were out of the question for most people.)

Initially, coach passengers flew coach planes, first class passengers flew first class planes, and each person on a particular flight paid the same price to be there. But in September 1955, TWA became the first airline to offer different cabins on the *same* plane, creating the modern version of a first class cabin and an economy cabin. They followed it up the next year with another successful innovation, the three-class cabin for international flights: "[sleeping] berths, fully-reclining sleeper seats with extended leg rests, and low-budget tourist seats."

The trend away from a flight having one price toward a flight having multiple prices continued to spread, and by 1961 more people were flying coach than first class. But it wasn't until 1978 that a major policy shift sent fares plunging: deregulation.

After Congress passed the Airline Deregulation Act, the CAB was soon dissolved and airlines were free to charge passengers whatever they wanted for flights. For years, flying had been a luxury product, even in coach. But as post-deregulation fares fell, flying became a transportation commodity, a fast and increasingly economical way to get from A to B.

1980S–PRESENT: DEMOCRATIZATION OF FLIGHTS AND NEW SOURCES OF REVENUE

With fares no longer set by a central board but determined instead by what airlines would sell and what travelers would pay, flying became significantly cheaper and more accessible for middle class Americans. New airlines popped up, including the first budget carriers, driving down the profitability of flying economy passengers.

In response, airlines sought to diversify their revenue streams. And it's worked. Their efforts to generate alternative income channels have been so successful that, even as a record number of people buy tickets, the majority of revenue for many airlines now comes from sources other than economy fares.

Here's how airlines make money today:

Airfare price discrimination. Rather than charging everyone on a flight the same fare, nowadays a single flight may have twenty or more fare options, accounting not just for the cabin you sit in but also whether your ticket includes checked baggage, whether it is eligible for a refund or an upgrade, how many frequent flyer miles it earns, and a variety of other factors. Generally speaking, the cheaper the fare, the more restrictions it has. The airlines' goal is to get as much money from each customer as he is willing to pay, something that would be impossible with a one-size-fits-all pricing method.

In addition to increased market segmentation, airfare pricing has become significantly more volatile. Flights used to cost the same, whether you booked six months or six hours ahead of time. Nowadays, airlines have developed complex algorithms that are constantly repricing airfare.

More premium seats sold. When commercial flights began, they were a luxury good, reserved exclusively for the upper crust. But beginning in 1948 and rapidly accelerating after deregulation, airlines shifted their focus toward economy tickets. They could fit far more economy seats on a plane, after all, and didn't have to pamper the occupants like first class passengers.

In the past decade that trend has begun to reverse itself, however, and airlines have focused instead on selling their most expensive seats. Take Delta. In 2011, just 9 percent of seats on their planes were premium. By 2019, they had increased that proportion to 24 percent. And as they added volume, they also did a *much* better job making money off their premium cabins. In 2011, Delta sold just 13 percent of their first class seats; in 2019, they sold 60 percent. (Delta is not alone; similar efforts are being made at American and United as well.) Rather than the old practice of indiscriminately handing out free upgrades, airlines now focus on profiting from premium seats via a combination of better price discrimination, corporate sales, and marketing to economy passengers fed up with cramped coach seats.

Consider this: Delta's overall revenue grew by $9 billion from 2011 through 2018—a 25 percent increase—despite the fact their economy ticket revenue went *down* by $1 billion. The Golden Age of Cheap Flights is taking place in economy class.

Credit cards and frequent flyer miles. In 1981, when American Airlines became the first major airline to launch a frequent flyer program, executives wouldn't have been able to predict that this innovation would one day become the difference between an airline that was profitable and one that wasn't. But that's precisely what's happened.

In 2018, American took in an average of 14.4 cents in revenue per available seat mile across all their flights but spent 14.9 cents while doing so. They *lost money* flying planes. What took 2018 from red to black, industry expert Gary Leff noted, was over $2 billion brought in by the airline's loyalty program, primarily through selling frequent flyer miles to banks, which dole them out to credit card holders. It's not just American; Delta and United also rake in billions annually through their loyalty programs and cobranded credit cards. Frequent flyer miles have become one of the strongest areas of revenue growth for airlines; airline analyst Joseph DeNardi predicted in 2019 that over half of the revenue airlines expect to generate over the next five years will come from selling miles.

Ownership in other airlines. Delta currently owns 49 percent of both Aeromexico and Virgin Atlantic and invests billions in partner airlines around the world. American has invested hundreds of millions in China Southern Airlines. United owns a portion of Brazilian airline Azul and is a creditor for Colombia's Avianca. Investments like these help U.S.-based airlines get a piece of the pie from travel growth in overseas markets.

Corporate contracts. It's hard to overstate just how important business travelers are for airlines. According to Yahoo journalist Ethan Klapper, corporate travelers account for approximately 12 percent of passengers on full-service airlines but 75 percent

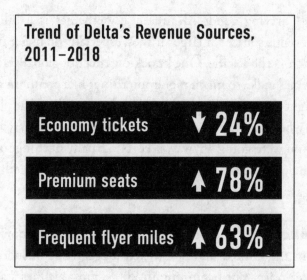

Trend of Delta's Revenue Sources, 2011–2018

Economy tickets	▼ 24%
Premium seats	▲ 78%
Frequent flyer miles	▲ 63%

of the revenue. The public saw just how lucrative corporate travelers can be in January 2019 when Twitter posts showing United's otherwise secret corporate accounts were accidentally made public. They revealed that United's largest corporate account, Apple, paid the airline $150 million annually, and a dozen other companies had similar contracts each worth over $10 million.

What was especially illuminating, though, was the information about United's San Francisco–Shanghai flights. Describing the route as "Our #1 market for Apple," the post noted that Apple paid $35 million annually for 50 business class seats a day on that route. When we wonder why an airline would offer $300 transoceanic economy tickets, it may be because a lucrative corporate contract induced them to operate that route. Even if not a single leisure traveler bought a United ticket from San Francisco to Shanghai, the airline would continue flying it because of Apple.

Cargo. Carrying goods in aircraft underbellies is a billion-dollar revenue source for large airlines, especially on major trade routes across the Pacific. One knock-on effect of global trade is that airlines make so much money on things like premium seats and freight that economy seats are sold cheap to fill up the plane. It's like when you drive home from college and a classmate hops a ride; you were going anyway, it costs virtually nothing for an additional passenger, and who knows—maybe they'll pitch in a bit for gas.

Add-on fees. For the first eighty years or so of commercial flights in the United States, checked luggage was included in the ticket price. But beginning in 2008, most airlines started charging passengers extra to check a bag. These fees have since become a massive revenue driver. In 2018, U.S. airlines collected approximately $5 billion in bag fees. They collected an additional $2.7 billion from reservation-change fees that year, and millions more from other ancillary fees like seat selection and onboard meals.

There's a hidden reason why airlines love add-on fees: They're taxed much lower than airfare. When you buy a domestic flight, the federal government levies a 7.5 percent excise tax on your fare, and airlines are required to include this tax in the fare they show you (rather than, say, the way stores don't show sales tax on the display price). Optional fees like bags and seat selection aren't included in the ticket price and thus aren't subject to the 7.5 percent excise tax. By no longer including bags in the ticket price, U.S. airlines saved $375 million in their 2018 taxes alone.

To sum up a century of commercial aviation economics, in the long term there's been a trend toward more price discrimination, and in the near term economy airfare has become less central to the airlines' bottom line.

But rather than just looking at airline economics from a high level, let's zoom in and see how these factors can impact what you'll pay for your next flight.

HOW AIRLINES CAN AFFORD TO SELL $300 ROUNDTRIP FLIGHTS TO EUROPE

As I type, American Airlines Flight 236 nonstop from New York City to Rome is offering economy seats for $271 roundtrip departing September 29 and returning October 6. It's on a Boeing 777 plane, which has 160 seats in economy, 55 seats in premium economy, and 45 seats in business class.

Though in reality fares are constantly jumping around, let's assume for simplicity's sake that (a) everyone in each section paid the same price to be there, and (b) every seat gets sold.

The 160 economy seats at $271 apiece would generate $43,360 in total revenue. The 55 premium economy seats, currently selling for $2,465, would bring in $135,575. And the 45 business class seats, selling for $5,071 each, would generate $228,195 in revenue. In other words, regular economy seats account for just 11 percent of the $400,000 American would yield in ticket sales. (Yes, this percentage would be a bit higher on most flights because it's rare to have a plane full of passengers who paid $271 roundtrip to Europe, but you see my point.)

It's not that American wouldn't love to charge more for their economy seats. They would! But raising their prices means that cheap flight lovers like you and me will just fly another airline that can get us to Rome for less (or not fly at all).

Airlines have figured out a business model in recent years that depends not on fickle, price-sensitive vacationers but, instead, on more reliable sources of income like premium travelers, banks, corporate contracts, and fees. In a sense, all these items are *subsidizing* economy fares, making $300 roundtrip flights to Europe possible.

Think of it like a restaurant. Not every item on the menu

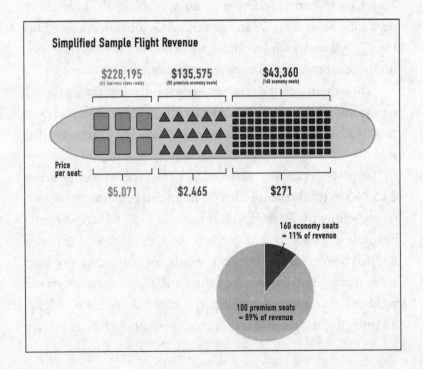

Simplified Sample Flight Revenue

$228,195 (45 business class seats) $135,575 (55 premium economy seats) $43,360 (160 economy seats)

Price per seat:

$5,071 $2,465 $271

160 economy seats = 11% of revenue

100 premium seats = 89% of revenue

has the same price markup. Economy seats are the steak, essentially sold at cost with just the barest of profit margins. Premium seats are the sodas, alcohol, and salads, marked up at huge profit. If the restaurant *only* sold steak, it would go out of business. The way it can afford to serve low-margin dishes is by generating high profits elsewhere. Airlines can still generate record profits even during a time like today—the Golden Age of Cheap Flights— when it's never been cheaper to fly.

KEY TAKEAWAYS

- Until recently, flying was so expensive that only the wealthy could afford it. But following deregulation in 1978—and accelerating in the 2010s—airfare became not only affordable but downright cheap.
- Airlines used to primarily make money selling coach tickets. Today, airlines generate a large and growing percentage of revenue from other sources like premium seats and frequent flyer miles.
- The fact that economy ticket revenue is less and less central to the airlines' bottom line is what allows them to slash prices on previously expensive long-haul flights.

6

THE GOLDEN AGE OF CHEAP FLIGHTS:
HOW AND WHY EVERYONE CAN NOW AFFORD TO FLY

IN 1914, THE WORLD'S FIRST FIXED-WING COMMERCIAL flight departed St. Petersburg, Florida, crossed the bay, and landed in Tampa 20 minutes later, a distance of about 23 miles. It had enough room for a single passenger, the former mayor of St. Petersburg, Abram C. Pheil, who paid $400 for the privilege—over $10,000 in 2019 dollars.

A century later, people are flying from Los Angeles to Shanghai—300 times farther than what Pheil flew—for a price 25 times cheaper.

It may come as little surprise that technologically driven services like air travel have gotten less expensive over the years. What many people miss, though, is just *how much* cheaper flying has become.

THE GREAT CHEAPENING

As we discussed in Chapter 5, for decades ticket prices were set by the Civil Aeronautics Board. Even if an airline wanted to, it was illegal to charge less than the fare set by the CAB. Though a lack of cheap flights hurt passengers, most large airlines opposed deregulation because they benefited from the status quo.

Let's look at two similar-length flights in the late 1970s: Boston to Washington, DC, and San Francisco to Los Angeles. Before deregulation, airfare on the former flight was set by the CAB at $60 each way. The San Francisco–Los Angeles flight, meanwhile, took place wholly within California and therefore wasn't subject to the CAB, which governed interstate flights. The fare was just $30.

When deregulation passed in 1978 over major airlines' objections, the result was exactly what proponents had predicted: Airfares began to plummet. It wasn't because airlines like TWA and Eastern wanted to charge passengers less, but because deregulation allowed new low-cost competitor airlines to enter the marketplace. Legacy airlines were *forced* to drop prices in order to compete.

Just how much ticket prices fell has been stunning. In the four decades since deregulation, average domestic airfare has dropped 50 percent in inflation-adjusted dollars. In 1981, the average domestic roundtrip flight cost $638 adjusted for inflation; in 2016, that figure had fallen to $367. And even that drop doesn't account for the fact that flights have gotten 25 percent longer on average over that timespan.

While the average airfare has been in free fall, what's especially heartening is how cheap the *least expensive* seats have become. Even as recently as the early 2010s, it was quite rare to see roundtrip flights from the United States to Europe for under

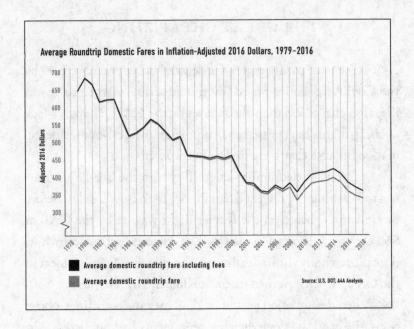

Average Roundtrip Domestic Fares in Inflation-Adjusted 2016 Dollars, 1979–2016

Average domestic roundtrip fare including fees

Average domestic roundtrip fare

Source: U.S. DOT; A4A Analysis

$700, and a $500 roundtrip flight was virtually unheard of. By the late 2010s, you could *regularly* find flights on full-service airlines to places like Barcelona or Paris for under $300 roundtrip.

You may be wondering: *What about all the fees airlines tack on nowadays? Are flights "cheap" only if you don't account for additional fees?*

In short, no. Even when adding on all the fees for bags, seat selection, and ticket changes we've collectively paid over the years—optional items that some people never use and others always do—flights are still far cheaper today than they used to be. (It's not just that flying has gotten cheaper; it's also gotten far better. As we'll explore in Chapter 9, despite nostalgia for the golden age of flying, the experience has significantly improved over the years.)

The drop in fares is especially stark when contrasting it with other consumer staples. Since 2000, prescription drug prices have increased at twice the rate of inflation, Disney World passes have more than tripled, and public college tuition and fees have more than quintupled. Flights, meanwhile, have gotten *cheaper* in real dollars, increasing at less than half the rate of inflation.

BOOKING CHEAP HOTELS/ACCOMMODATIONS

Whenever I'm going on vacation, these are the four sites and two tactics I use to search for a place to stay:

- Google Hotels: A new entrant in the hotel booking scene, but a fast and powerful site that offers a far better user experience than most other online travel agencies.
- Airbnb/Vrbo: Especially affordable when I'm looking to stay in the center of town, where hotels are often cringingly expensive.
- Roomer: A site where you can buy other people's nonrefundable accommodations for a fraction of what they paid.
- RedWeek: Similar to Roomer but for timeshare bookings.
- Prepaying: If you're confident your plans won't change, you can often save 20 percent or more by prepaying for a hotel rather than booking a refundable stay.
- Booking directly: Because hotels pay large commissions to online travel agencies (as much as 30 percent), they're often willing to give a sizable

discount to travelers who book directly. Sometimes contracts with travel agencies forbid hotels from publicly offering lower rates, but if you call a hotel directly and ask if they'll offer a lower rate over the phone, many will.

What's remarkable is how few people know that fares have gotten significantly cheaper. In 2015, as fares were plummeting, a Gallup poll found that just 51 percent of Americans who had taken a flight in the past year were satisfied with their ticket price. A 2018 Morning Consult poll found that just 13 percent correctly identified that the recent cost of airfare has gotten better.

There's a number of factors that could be causing this widespread misconception. It may be a lack of understanding about inflation. A $350 flight in 2016 is relatively cheaper than a $300 flight in 2000, even though it may sound more expensive. Another possibility is anchoring, the cognitive bias we discussed in Chapter 1 to become overly attached to an initial piece of data. Perhaps you last went to Europe five years ago and paid $1,000 for your flight. It'd be easy to unwittingly assume that's simply the going rate to reach Europe. And finally, few among us are flight experts. Most people overpay for flights and, as a result, assume they're expensive.

WHY ARE FLIGHTS SO CHEAP NOW?

There are eight principle factors that have been driving down airfare since deregulation in the late 1970s, especially so in the past few years: competition, price discrimination, cheap oil,

densification, more efficient planes, government subsidies, corporate contracts, and ancillary revenues.

Let's consider each individually.

Competition

The single biggest force applying downward pressure on airfare
is competition from other airlines. Most travelers treat flights
like a commodity; surveys show that once someone has a trip in
mind, the most important factor driving their purchasing decision isn't the schedule or the airline but the price.

A plethora of new airlines like People Express popped up in
the wake of deregulation, undercutting legacy airlines and helping drive down fares nationwide. Some airlines like American
and Delta were able to successfully adapt, improving their service and cutting their fares to compete. Others, like TWA and
Pan American, lost too many travelers to new airlines and soon
folded or were acquired.

Two analysts, Daniel M. Kasper and Darin Lee, studied
how competition has impacted the airline industry. They found
that "continued growth of lower cost carriers and the expansion
by all carriers at competitors' hubs has resulted in fare levels
among the lowest in U.S. aviation history."

The phenomenon of budget airlines driving down fares in a
new market is colloquially known as the "Southwest Effect." According to Kasper and Lee, "In 2016, Southwest's presence on a
route lowered fares by more than 21 percent." And it's not just
Southwest; on average fares drop 25 percent when JetBlue enters
a new market, 24 percent with Alaska, and 19 percent with Spirit.

How are budget airlines able to offer substantially cheaper fares? They have a number of competitive advantages, including lower labor costs, newer planes that are more fuel-efficient and require less maintenance, lower operating costs, fewer expensive legacy costs like outdated computer systems, fleet consistency so they only need pilots and crew who can operate one or a small number of plane types, and more nimble decision making. Lower costs across the board allow them to offer lower fares.

Over the past couple of decades, budget airlines have grown rapidly. According to Kasper and Lee, low-cost carriers like Spirit and Frontier "have captured nearly all of the growth in domestic demand since 2007." In 1997, budget airlines and small carriers accounted for just 23 percent of domestic passengers. Every single year for the next two decades, however, that share has increased. By 2016, they accounted for 46 percent of domestic passengers.

It's not just competition with new budget airlines but also among older legacy airlines. In the past decade especially, airlines have embraced the tactic of attacking each other's hubs (more on this in Chapter 7). During the 2010s, United enjoyed massive growth in Delta's Atlanta hub, American expanded significantly in Delta's Salt Lake City hub, and Delta grew substantially in American's Dallas/Fort Worth and Charlotte hubs. This increased competition across the board is helping bring down fares for millions of travelers.

Competition with foreign carriers has been driving down fares as well. Over the past decade, international airlines have been steadily increasing their capacity on U.S.-bound flights. A new chapter began in 2013 when Norwegian Airlines, a

European-based budget carrier, started flying to the United States, offering fares under $300 roundtrip, a price unheard of at the time. Norwegian grew so quickly that within five years, it had unseated British Airways as the largest non-U.S. airline flying to New York City.

Price Discrimination

As we noted in Chapter 5, beginning after World War II and accelerating after deregulation, airlines have used price discrimination as their business model for selling tickets. In 1947, every New Yorker flying roundtrip to Geneva, for instance, paid $746 ($8,569 today) for their ticket. But soon thereafter, airlines began offering different fares for the same route, depending on amenities.

Before deregulation, fares were highly correlated with distance. The farther a plane flew, the more jet fuel it needed, so the more each passenger paid for a ticket. But after deregulation, as airlines became more complex and started making money in new ways, airfare began decoupling from distance. Distance traveled is still a factor that influences airfare, but it's no longer the only, or even main, component. For example, I just searched for fares on two nonstop routes in mid-September. Flights from New York City to Pittsburgh, a distance of 335 miles, ran $177 roundtrip on Delta. Meanwhile, Delta was selling flights from New York City to Fort Lauderdale, 1,076 miles apart, for $117 roundtrip.

Economy fares have gotten cheaper because rather than charging for miles flown, airlines nowadays rely on charging more to price-insensitive travelers (say, businesspeople) and less to price-sensitive travelers (say, young vacationers). Generating more revenue elsewhere has allowed airlines to slash fares for the cheap flight aficionados of the world.

Cheap Oil

Amidst turmoil in the Middle East, Hurricane Katrina, fears of dwindling petroleum reserves, and zealous speculative commodities traders in the mid-2000s, oil hit an all-time high of $147 per barrel in July 2008.

The price of oil is no small matter for airlines. Jet fuel is normally an airline's second largest expense after labor, but it became the top cost after the 2008 price spike. With oil prices in summer 2008 double what they were a year earlier, airlines had no choice but to hike fares substantially. (The episode also prompted airlines to lose billions betting on the price of oil and, in Delta's case, purchase an oil refinery.)

However, as the financial crisis took hold, oil prices plunged 70 percent in a matter of months. Since 2015, the price has remained well under $80 per barrel, nowhere near its record high. Given how dependent airlines are on jet fuel, it's little surprise that the decrease in prices has coincided with the ongoing Golden Age of Cheap Flights.

Densification

It's not your imagination: Airplane seats really *have* gotten smaller over the years. In the past few decades, average seat width has narrowed by nearly two inches, and average seat pitch (the distance from the back of one seat to the back of the next seat) has shrunk by more than three inches. The goal isn't so much sadism (but maybe?) as it is cramming more people on board and boosting the amount of revenue each flight generates. Increasing the supply of available seats, meanwhile, puts downward pressure on fares.

Better Planes

Newer planes are helping drive down fares in a few ways. First, they're more fuel-efficient. Like cars, newer planes get better fuel economy than older planes. For example, Boeing's 787 Dreamliner, which began commercial service in 2011, is 20 percent more fuel-efficient than the 767 model, which debuted in the 1980s. As newer, better planes enter circulation, old gas-guzzlers get phased out.

Second, more efficient planes allow for new routes between smaller distant cities. If jumbo jets like the double-decker Airbus A380 were the only ones with enough fuel capacity to cross the Atlantic, then only routes with the highest traffic levels (think New York City–London and Chicago–Paris) could be sustained. New, smaller planes like the Airbus A350 (which holds half the passengers of an A380) allow airlines to fly long-haul secondary routes at a profit.

Government Subsidies

Many airlines around the world receive significant financial support from governments, in the form of either funding or outright ownership. For example, according to the Centre for Aviation, over a billion dollars in government subsidies went to four prominent Chinese airlines in 2014, helping drive up visitor numbers in secondary cities like Chengdu. These subsidies, which make it cheaper for passengers to fly to and from China, are putting the Asian nation on pace to surpass the United States as the world's largest aviation market around 2022.

Subsidies are not unique to China. Major Middle Eastern carriers receive billions in government funding, as do dozens of other airlines around the world, from South Africa to India to Italy and beyond. Even U.S. airlines receive a significant amount of government support, including tax breaks and the Essential Air Service program, which subsidizes airlines serving more than 150 small and rural communities around the country.

Corporate Contracts

As discussed in Chapter 5, on some flights, the most valuable revenue driver is not normal ticketed passengers but the businesspeople sitting up front. Corporate contracts (including shipping cargo) can make it profitable for airlines to fly flights that would be unprofitable if they were making money only off leisure travelers. A $300 roundtrip economy ticket from California to China would be impracticable if airlines weren't making millions hauling electronics and executives.

Ancillary Revenues

Another factor driving fares down is the recent trend of unbundling—that is, no longer including some perks in the overall ticket price. Before 2008, almost all major airlines automatically included checked bags with your ticket. After 2008, checked bags began costing extra, and soon fees for other add-ons like advance seat selection emerged.

It's not just add-on fees that are providing ancillary revenue and driving down fares; it's other add-on vacation items as well. Airlines make large commissions selling hotel rooms and car rentals to their passengers. Tickets that are geared toward vacationers—say, flights to Hawaii, or fares booked many months in advance—are sometimes sold at a loss in the hopes of generating additional revenue after the passenger has booked. In this approach, selling cheap flights early has the benefit of giving the airline more time to sell that passenger more stuff. Economy tickets are the steak, and the airline would like to know if you'd like salad and wine as well.

It's a bit surprising, considering how common air travel has become, that few people recognize that flying is getting cheaper. In 1965, fewer than 20 percent of Americans had ever flown. Fifty years later, over 80 percent have taken a flight, including about half of all Americans in any given year. That level of market penetration would have been impossible if it still cost thousands of dollars to fly coast to coast, much less internationally.

Expensive tickets still exist. Go take a look at what it costs to fly first class to Sydney. But airfare has dropped significantly on average, and, more important, the cheapest fares have gotten way cheaper. Ignoring—or denying—the reality that flights are getting cheaper is an expensive mistake, one that's unfortunately all too common.

Now that we understand why flights have become so cheap, there's another matter we need to explore before we can feel truly confident planning a trip: why airfare is always changing.

KEY TAKEAWAYS

- We are living in the Golden Age of Cheap Flights. It's never been cheaper to fly than it is today, even accounting for add-on fees. But most people incorrectly believe that flying is getting more, not less, expensive.
- Eight primary factors are driving fares downward: competition, price discrimination, cheap oil, densification, better planes, government subsidies, corporate contracts, and ancillary revenues.
- The growth of budget airlines in particular is helping reduce fares across the board, a phenomenon known as the Southwest Effect. Even if you never fly budget airlines, they're driving down airfare on legacy airlines as well.

7

UNPREDICTABLE AND IRRATIONAL: WHY AIRFARE IS SO VOLATILE

W HENEVER I'M ASKED A QUESTION LIKE "WHAT DOES IT cost to fly from Houston to Amsterdam?" I feel like I've just been posed a riddle.

Do I pull out my phone and quote the current lowest price anytime over the next twelve months? Or should I ask the specific time of year they're hoping for, if not specific dates? Should I note the current cheapest fare is via Istanbul, approximately double the length of a direct flight? Perhaps I ought to mention how every month or so the fare tends to drop below $450 roundtrip, but only for a day or two. Would I be remiss if I left out the time there was a $246 roundtrip mistake fare, even though those fares are unpredictable and this one was back in 2016? And no matter what price I tell them, there's a decent chance the fare will have changed in a few hours. Should I ask for the person's contact information so I can get in touch?

As we discussed earlier, it's a common mistake to think of buying airfare the way we think of buying bagels. Bagels are consistent and logical; the price fluctuates very little and depends primarily on how many you buy. Airfare, meanwhile, is turbulent, unpredictable, and most people on a given flight paid vastly different prices to be there.

It didn't used to be this way. For decades prior to deregulation, airfare had a singular price: whatever the Civil Aeronautics Board set it at. And though fares were stable, they were also exorbitant. Since deregulation, though, airlines have been free to price how they wish. The result: much cheaper, and much more volatile, airfare.

A frequent mistake people make is to assume that airfare always increases or decreases gradually. In fact, wild price swings are commonplace. In mid-March 2018, fares from Atlanta to Amsterdam were parked around $900 roundtrip for flights in September. On March 26, though, prices dropped to $401 roundtrip in a Big Europe Sale (more on those shortly). Three days later, fares on that route fell even further, to $346 roundtrip. And about thirty-six hours after that, they shot up to $1,350 roundtrip. The exact same ticket on the exact same flight had a thousand-dollar price difference in a matter of days. Glory and sunshine to thee who booked a $346 Europe flight on March 30; gnashing of teeth to those who booked on March 31.

This degree of oscillation isn't abnormal. A CheapAir.com analysis of one domestic flight found that it changed price 135 times during the nearly 12 months it was available for purchase, or about once every 2.4 days. Sometimes it would go weeks without changing, and in other instances it would change multiple times a day.

While airline revenue managers consider dozens of constantly changing factors to help them determine airfare, from oil prices to worldwide events to major economic trends, there are three primary causes for price fluctuations: autopilot pricing, unexpected customer demand, and competition.

Autopilot pricing: Though an airline may have only three cabins on a plane, each cabin has many different prices, known as fare buckets, available at a given moment. A 150-seat plane going from Seattle to Denver may have 10 economy seats available for $130 roundtrip, 20 available for $150 roundtrip, 30 available for $200 roundtrip, and so forth. The number of seats available in any given fare bucket isn't a secret but it is obscured; all we typically see when we search Expedia is the lowest available price. So if I searched for flights from Seattle to Denver on Monday, saw a fare for $130, then searched again on Tuesday and saw a fare for $150, it may not have been the airline increasing prices but, rather, tickets in the cheapest fare bucket selling out.

In addition, most fares have restrictions in their fine print about how far in advance they must be purchased. For example, the $130 roundtrip Seattle–Denver ticket may require the traveler to book at least three weeks before traveling. If you're booking just a week before travel, the cheapest eligible fare may be double that price, and a day before it may be triple or more.

As one airline revenue manager noted, "The majority of fare changes aren't really changes on our part: they happen because people are purchasing up inventory at the lowest published fare or the advance purchase restrictions are kicking in."

Unexpected customer demand: Airlines have developed complex algorithms that look at past ticket sales and other factors to predict how many seats they can sell at various prices on any given route. But if the algorithm predicted an airline would sell 50 percent of Atlanta–Amsterdam coach seats at $900 by four months before departure, and in reality they've only sold 20 percent, a revenue manager may decide to manually drop the price in order to sell more seats.

Competition: Airfare pricing decisions would be far simpler if airlines didn't have to contend with half a dozen or more other competitors on any given route. Thankfully for travelers, airlines have to constantly be aware of their competitors' prices, knowing that most travelers are not loyal to one airline but instead are loyal to the cheapest flight (as we should be). If United is selling flights from New York City to Los Angeles for $300 roundtrip, and Delta drops their price on the route to $230 roundtrip, chances are United will quickly match Delta's fares in order to not lose out on market share. Sometimes this will involve attacking each other's hubs, offering cheaper fares out of a competitor's hub airport in order to lure away travelers who had been loyal to the hometown airline. For instance, at 1 p.m. on November 27, 2018, American began selling $314 roundtrip flights to Honolulu out of Houston, a United hub. By 3 p.m., United had responded by selling $314 roundtrip flights to Honolulu out of American's Dallas hub. In some hub attacks, both airlines drop prices in their own hubs as well, and cheap flight lovers everywhere rejoice.

As I've monitored airfare for Scott's Cheap Flights over the past five years, every month or so these factors come together like Captain Planet's rings to produce what we call a Big Europe Sale.

A Big Europe Sale is when flights from a large number of U.S. airports to a handful of European airports go on deep discount, typically below $550 roundtrip and sometimes closer to

$400 roundtrip. The specific number of airports included varies from sale to sale. In its largest iteration, a Big Europe Sale can include virtually every U.S. airport with commercial service and four dozen or more European destinations. Oftentimes when this happens, cities get priced in lockstep, such as a July 2019 sale from 132 U.S. airports to Germany, almost all priced at $355 roundtrip, whether flying out of Fort Wayne or San Diego. Though this type of sale primarily occurs with flights to Europe, occasionally it will happen with other destinations like Australia or East Asia.

Nationwide deals like a Big Europe Sale aren't announced or advertised. Airlines don't need to run ads to convince residents in Cody, Wyoming, or Asheville, North Carolina, to jump on $500 Europe flights; they're used to seeing fares over $1,500 roundtrip. Those tickets sell themselves. By quietly slashing fares, airline revenue managers give themselves flexibility to monitor how quickly tickets are getting scooped up and end the sale when they're ready. (This is also why Big Europe Sales often happen on evenings and weekends, to limit the deluge of customers before they pull the sale.)

Big Europe Sales happen as a way for airline revenue managers to get rid of seats they're having more trouble selling than expected, usually for travel dates two to eight months out. You might be wondering why revenue managers don't wait until closer to departure date to put those tickets on sale. The problem is that most leisure travelers, especially for international trips, prefer booking their flights at least a few months ahead of time. If airlines were to slash prices on last-minute tickets, they'd risk eating into the high prices that business travelers, who tend to book late, are happy to pay.

Whether during a Big Europe Sale or on other routes, airlines tend to match one another's fares because they know that when consumers look at flights, price is the most important factor driving their purchase. A 2018 Morning Consult poll found that 74 percent of Americans surveyed said price was "very important" when it comes to buying tickets. Just 26 percent said they would be willing to pay a premium in order to fly a preferred airline. With this in mind, one airline's fare change can have a ripple effect across the industry.

Take Lufthansa, which has to compete with budget carriers like Ryanair on many of its routes. "We do not sell tickets in Europe for 35 euros one-way for simply profitability reasons," Chief Commercial Officer Harry Hohmeister said at a company presentation. Instead, they begrudgingly match these fares, and lose money in the short term, in order to retain customer loyalty. If they don't match the cheapest fares available, they risk losing some of their most valuable customers to competitors.

Though there's no singular price for any given route, that doesn't mean airfare is a complete mystery. On the contrary, there are a number of predictable factors that determine airfare. With a firm understanding of how airlines think about setting ticket prices, we can use that knowledge to never overpay for flights again.

HOW FLIGHT PRICES ARE DETERMINED

One of the most common misperceptions in travel is that the price of a flight depends on how far you fly.

As the thinking goes, short flights are always cheap and long flights are always expensive because the short flights require less fuel and long flights need more. A ten-hour drive is more expensive than a two-hour drive; why should flying be any different?

Prior to deregulation, this was indeed the pricing model. Airfare was determined almost entirely by trip length, typically at a rate of about six cents per mile. But nowadays, distance is just one among many factors, and it's hardly the most important one. Remember, it's more expensive to fly to Jamaica than to China. And flights to a nearby small city are often more expensive than flights to a distant big city.

Instead of thinking about distance, the better mental model for predicting airfare is competition among airlines.

Flights between airports where a lot of airlines compete for travelers—say, New York City to Chicago—tend to be relatively inexpensive. If you're flying to or from a city where one airline has a monopoly—say Minneapolis (Delta) or Phoenix (American)—cheap flights are somewhat less common. If you're flying into or out of a small airport, especially one with service on just a single airline, there's no competition putting downward pressure on fares, so they tend to be pricey.

Do note that these are general rules, and exceptions pop up frequently depending on the specific route, airline, time of year, and a host of other factors. Flights from San Francisco to Chicago are usually cheaper than flights from San Francisco to Milwaukee, except occasionally when they're not. Flights to London are usually cheaper than flights to Edinburgh, except occasionally when they're not. Think of it like betting on a favorite in sports: Just because one team is favored to win doesn't mean there's never an upset.

Airlines' pricing model is largely based on a single principle: achieving maximum willingness to pay from each passenger. If a passenger *needs* to take a certain flight and would pay whatever cost, an airline has left money on the table if they charge that passenger $200 rather than $2,000.

To that end, one of the most important objectives for airlines is distinguishing between business travelers and leisure travelers. Business travelers tend to have a high willingness to pay because their company foots the bill, and it's hard to justify missing an important meeting because you were hoping for a cheap flight that never came. Business travelers have low flexibility and low price-sensitivity.

Leisure travelers, meanwhile, tend to care a lot about the price because they have limited cash to spend on travel, and there is less rigidity in their travel dates. Vacationers have high flexibility and high price-sensitivity.

Airlines want to charge different prices to business travelers and vacationers. Even more than that, they want to charge vacationers with low flexibility and/or low price-sensitivity more than vacationers who can travel anytime but need a cheap flight. The tricky part for airlines is figuring out who's who.

How can an airline determine a given traveler's willingness to pay? They could try asking, but humans have a well-established propensity to lie, particularly when there's a financial benefit to do so. Instead, the best solution airlines have come up with is to charge more for the *types* of fares that business travelers and people with a high willingness to pay tend to prefer.

Here are factors that business travelers and people with low flexibility tend to prefer, and thus airlines charge more for:

BUSINESS & PRICE-INSENSITIVE TRAVELERS LIKE:	
ADVANCE BOOKING	Last-minute bookings
TRAVEL DAYS	Monday, Friday
TRIP LENGTH	Under 7 days
CLASS OF SERVICE	Business, premium economy
FLEXIBILITY	Changes, cancellations allowed
ROUTING	Nonstop
ELITE STATUS BENEFITS	Yes
CHECKED BAGGAGE	Included
ABILITY TO UPGRADE	Yes
TIME OF YEAR	Peak summer and holidays
ONE-WAY FLIGHTS	Yes

Price-sensitive travelers, meanwhile, can increase their chances of finding a deal by avoiding flights with the in-demand characteristics that business travelers and wealthy people prefer.

INCREASED LIKELIHOOD OF CHEAP FLIGHTS	
ADVANCE BOOKING	Months in advance
TRAVEL DAYS	Tuesday, Wednesday, Saturday
TRIP LENGTH	7 days or more
CLASS OF SERVICE	Main economy, basic economy
FLEXIBILITY	Changes, cancellations not allowed or require a fee

Routing	Connecting
Elite status benefits	Limited
Checked baggage	Costs extra
Ability to upgrade	Limited
Time of year	Off-peak
One-way flights (international)	No

To be clear, none of these factors by itself is prohibitive. Sometimes direct routes are cheapest, sometimes peak summer deals pop up, sometimes cheap Friday flights are available. But in general, the factors that business travelers prefer are the ones that airlines charge more for because they've reasoned (correctly) that businesses will pay up.

Let's take a closer look at one of these factors: trip length. Business travelers who spend the work week separated from their families are eager to get home for the weekend, so their trips are usually fewer than seven days. Vacationers, meanwhile, want to maximize time spent at a destination relative to the time spent getting there. Not many people want to spend just a day or two in Europe if they had to spend a day on each end in flight.

With these two types of travelers in mind, airlines attach different fare rules to each ticket. The cheapest tickets on a route often include requirements like a minimum 7-day trip or an overnight Saturday stay at the destination before taking the return flight. In doing so, airlines are trying to ensure that business travelers with big budgets aren't getting the cheap fares intended for leisure travelers. (This is also why many one-way flights, particularly international ones, are exorbitantly expensive; the airline has no idea when you'll return and therefore has to ensure you're not a business traveler trying to get around the minimum-stay fare rules.)

Airline revenue managers will set aside a certain number of seats in each fare bucket based on what they think they can sell. Take United Flight 2248 from Portland, Oregon, to Newark on a Tuesday in October. At the time of writing, the airline has tickets available in 25 different fare buckets. The cheapest bucket, N, is a basic economy fare and costs $119. The N fare comes with a host of restrictions in exchange for the cheapest rate, including reduced frequent flyer mileage earning; no full-size carry-on or checked bag included; no ability to upgrade, change, or cancel the ticket; no advanced seat selection; and low priority order in case of overbooking or flight disruptions. The $264 economy ticket in fare bucket L, meanwhile, is a refundable fare that offers standard mileage earning, a full-size carry-on, advance seat assignment, ability to upgrade, and a higher priority placement in case of travel disruptions. Despite a stark price difference, both are economy fares on the same flight. The people who buy them may even end up as seatmates.

There will always be an element of unpredictability to airfare. Like the weather, you can be confident in some macro trends (it will snow in Chicago this winter) without precisely knowing some micro trends (whether it will snow in Chicago on January 14). But the more you avoid the types of tickets business travelers like—hewing instead to the fares airlines intend for leisure travelers—the better your likelihood of coming across a cheap flight. And the more you remember airfare is volatile, not static, the less tempted you'll be to settle for a bad fare.

After all, if the flight you want is expensive today, your best bet is often to wait. Today's price may have little predictive power of tomorrow's price.

Once you've mastered thinking like a leisure traveler, how do you go about actually *getting* cheap flights? Using the Flight First Method and shunning business-oriented flights is crucial from a theoretical perspective, but now we need to start putting those principles into practice: where you should search, when you should book, how to avoid pernicious fees, how to think about budget airlines and basic economy. In short, how can you avoid overpaying for flights?

KEY TAKEAWAYS

- There's no single price to fly a given route. Instead, airfare is highly volatile, prone to wild and unpredictable swings. These price changes are largely driven by three factors: autopilot pricing, changes in customer demand, and competition among airlines.
- How far you fly has only a small correlation with what you can expect to pay. A far more important factor in determining airfare is how much competition there is among the airlines on a given route.
- Airlines try to charge more for the types of fares business travelers purchase and less for the types of fares leisure travelers purchase. Booking well in advance, traveling midweek, and taking a 7-day trip are all variables that tend to produce cheaper fares, though there are frequently exceptions to the rule.

8

THE FUNDAMENTALS: ANSWERS TO EVERYDAY FLIGHT-BOOKING QUESTIONS

NOW THAT WE HAVE A CLEAR SENSE OF HOW PRIORITIZing cheap flights can transform your life, let's explore the nitty-gritty of how to get them: where to book, which destinations are often cheap, which aren't, how to avoid those nasty add-on fees, what's the deal with basic economy. This chapter will demystify some of your most common yet vexing travel questions.

The tactics in this chapter aren't by themselves sufficient to master cheap flights; to accomplish that requires an overhaul of the way we *think* about planning vacations. But there are a handful of basic decisions that must be made with every vacation booking, and poor execution risks eating away at the savings and joy you'd accumulated by optimizing for cheap flights.

WHERE SHOULD I BOOK MY FLIGHTS?

Here's an industry secret that few are willing to admit (often because it's in their financial interest to claim otherwise): There's no single cheapest place to book flights.

Few online travel agencies—sites like Orbitz or Expedia—will concede this, of course. They have many fine marketers working long hours to convince you that they alone have the cheapest fares. But as someone who's spent years sifting through millions of fares across hundreds of airlines and online travel agencies (OTAs), I implore you: Don't believe them.

It's not that there's never price variation among OTAs; on the contrary, there almost always is, at least at the margins. The issue is that no single airline or OTA consistently has the best price on airfare. OTAs are like gas stations trying to convince you that their gas—which looks, smells, and costs the same—is somehow superior to gas at the station across the street.

When thinking about where to book flights online, there are three categories of sites: airlines, OTAs, and flight search engines. Each has its advantages and drawbacks to consider.

Airlines

Airline websites are straightforward: You can search for flights and book your ticket directly from the carrier. You'll only see fares for that airline and their partners.

There are a few benefits to booking directly. First, when you book on an airline's website, your ticket gets issued almost immediately. In certain circumstances, this can be a key advantage.

Any delay from the moment you hit PURCHASE means there's a chance the fare you booked is no longer available by the time your ticket is issued. While OTAs typically issue tickets within a few minutes of purchase, delays are not unheard of. Especially if you've found a mistake fare that could disappear at a moment's notice, maximizing speed is important.

Second, you're protected by the 24-hour rule only if you book directly with the airline. The 24-hour rule is a Department of Transportation regulation that automatically gives travelers a 24-hour grace period after purchase during which they can cancel their ticket and get a full refund without any penalties or fees.*

Every flight booking, even on foreign airlines, is protected by the 24-hour rule so long as it meets a few conditions:

- The flight is to, from, or within the United States.
- The flight is at least a week from departure.
- The fare was booked directly with an airline (not through an online travel agency).

Third, booking directly with an airline can be helpful if there are any changes or mishaps with your itinerary. If a hailstorm cancels your connecting flight, or you decide that visiting Houston in mid-August no longer seems as wise as it did when you booked, altering your itinerary is quite a bit simpler when your ticket was issued by the airline rather than a middleman.

---

* The regulation allows airlines to choose between offering a 24-hour hold or a 24-hour refund window. Currently, all U.S. airlines have opted to offer the latter.

Online Travel Agencies

OTAs are third-party sellers. There are a handful of major OTAs you've heard of and hundreds of minor OTAs you may not have. When you book a flight through an OTA, it serves as an intermediary, accepting payment from you and processing your ticket request with the airline.

TOP OTAS

- Expedia
- Priceline
- Orbitz

The primary benefit of booking through OTAs is that, rather than showing you fares only from a single airline, they allow you to compare fares across dozens of carriers. Flight prices are usually about the same as booking directly with the airline, though on occasion OTAs are cheaper.

If you need a hotel or rental car, OTAs sometimes offer savings by bundling these bookings together, but the discount isn't always substantial. OTAs will also try to engender loyalty by offering their own rewards programs (in my experience, the discounts have always been too paltry and complicated to warrant consistently booking with the same OTA).

The drawbacks of booking with an OTA mirror the benefits of booking directly with an airline. There can be a delay in issuing your ticket, and your selected fare might not be available anymore; you could run into issues if any itinerary changes are needed due to cancellations or weather; and you're not protected by the federal 24-hour rule.

Although a handful of major OTAs like Orbitz and Priceline offer their own 24-hour rule protections, it's not the same as booking directly. OTA 24-hour guarantees aren't useless—in some situations they can actually be more expansive by offering a longer refund window over the weekend, for example—but they're less reliable. That's because booking through an OTA doesn't offer the same legal protection you automatically receive by booking directly with an airline. Indeed, there are a number of reports from travelers who tried to cancel within 24 hours of booking through an OTA, only to be put on hold for hours and finding themselves outside the refund window by the time they reached an agent.

BOOKING CHEAP CAR RENTALS

Although there's no one site that's always cheapest to book flights, from what I've seen there is a cheapest place for car rentals: Costco Travel. If you've got a Costco membership, be sure to check their travel site's car-rental page, as they consistently have the lowest rates, as well as waived fees for an additional driver.

To truly get the lowest price, be sure to recheck the rates periodically. Unlike flights, there's no fee to cancel car rentals, so if the new price is lower than your original booking, just cancel and rebook to pocket the savings. This is precisely what happened on my last three rentals, and I saved anywhere from $25 to $150 off my original booking.

There's also a difference between major OTAs and smaller OTAs. While most OTAs perform their basic function just fine—exchanging your money for a ticket—there are differences in customer service quality. Big OTAs invest much more in support, which comes in handy if you need to change or cancel your flight. Smaller OTAs tend to underinvest in customer service in order to pass the savings along and offer even lower fares. Whether you'd prefer to pay more and get better service or pay less and risk worse service is a personal decision, but it is important to recognize the trade-offs and be clear-eyed about which is best for your situation.

One thing to note about OTAs is that many have *terrible* online reviews. I personally take these with a grain of salt. It's not that I consider them to have no value; on the contrary, other travelers' experiences can be instructive. It's the nature of online reviews, though, that gives me pause. How many people book a trip through an OTA, take an uneventful flight, and then feel motivated to go back and write a review? Probably a much lower percentage than people who had a negative experience and are eager to vent.

Flight Search Engines

Flight search engines are similar to OTAs in that they compare fares across many airlines, but there's one major difference: You can't actually book tickets through them. Instead, they do metasearches of OTAs and airlines in order to show you the best possible fares for a given route, saving you the hassle of searching each airline and OTA individually.

TOP FLIGHT SEARCH ENGINES

- Google Flights
- Kayak
- Skyscanner
- Momondo

However, not all flight search engines generate the same results. Google Flights, for instance, draws its airfares solely from airlines and a few major OTAs like Expedia and Orbitz. Momondo, meanwhile, searches many smaller OTAs as well.

One important caveat: Southwest Airlines' fares don't currently show up on any OTA or flight search engine. Their fares are found only on their website.

With three different places to look for flights—airline websites, OTAs, and flight search engines—how should a cheap flight aficionado go about weighing where to book their tickets?

There are two similar but distinct components here: where to find and where to buy. (And in case it wasn't clear, where you search and where you book don't have to be the same place.) Let's first explore the best way to search for cheap flights.

Fortunately, there's a straightforward answer here: Flight search engines are the best place to find cheap flights. They save a lot of time during the search process and ensure you'll see the cheapest fares available.

Though there are many flight search engines, my personal favorite is a relatively new one: Google Flights. (In case there was any doubt, I don't get any commission, compensation, kickbacks, good vibes, goodwill, or anything at all for my recommendations. My loyalty is to cheap flights, and cheap flights alone.) Like other flight search engines, Google Flights' meta-search combs through an array of OTAs; its true advantage is the user experience. Most sites limit your search to one specific origin city and one specific destination. Google Flights lets users input up to 7 origin airports and up to 7 destination airports, 49 possible routes in total. It even lets users input a country or continent as the destination, showing where the cheapest flights are across an entire region.

Let's say you live in Philadelphia and want to visit Europe. A typical flight search engine will restrict your search to flights departing Philadelphia and arriving in one specific European airport, say Barcelona. If you're also interested in fares to Madrid, you'd need to search again.

Using Google Flights, though, you could set as your departure airport not just Philadelphia, but also six other airports that are a short train ride away—three in the New York City area and three in the Washington, DC, area. For your destination, you could include Barcelona, Madrid, and up to five more airports. Google Flights will take those inputs and show you the cheapest possible fares among those 49 possible routes, not just for a specific date or two but across the entire 12-month calendar.

We discussed in Chapter 3 the importance of setting cheap flights as your top priority. No other flight search engine or OTA makes it as easy as Google Flights to quickly sift through thousands of options and home in on the single cheapest flight.

While Google Flights excels in robustness, flexibility, and speed, one drawback is that it can sometimes miss cheaper fares if they're found only on smaller OTAs. Best practice, therefore, is to start your search on Google Flights, locate the cheapest route and dates that appeal to you, and then check that flight on a site like Skyscanner or Momondo to see if there's a lower possible price.

For example, in mid-2019 the Scott's Cheap Flights team found a deal from Los Angeles to Shanghai. On Google Flights, the fare for a February 20–27 trip was listed as $319 roundtrip on five-star Hainan Airlines, bookable on Orbitz, Priceline, or directly with the airline. The same search on Skyscanner, though, gave a fare of $280 roundtrip, bookable through a smaller OTA, Hop2. Whether it's worth an extra $39 to avoid a minor OTA is up to you.

WHERE TO BOOK CHEAP FLIGHTS

All things equal, it's better to book directly with an airline than through an OTA, for three reasons: You don't risk the fare disappearing while you wait for your ticket to be issued, you're covered by the 24-hour rule, and it's much simpler in case your itinerary ends up needing to be changed.

The price isn't always equal, though. Sometimes OTAs are cheaper, or perhaps you're offered significant savings by bundling a rental car and/or hotel as well.

BOOKING CHEAPER TICKETS ONE AT A TIME

When you're traveling with a group, instead of just searching for the entire group, see if fares are cheaper by booking one or two tickets at a time.

In summer 2019, I searched for three passengers from Portland to New York. Google Flights showed a one-way fare of $178 per ticket, an okay but not great price. When I reduced the number of passengers to two, though, the price dropped to $117 per person. I booked those two tickets at $117, then booked the third ticket at $178, resulting in a total cost of $412 rather than the original $534.

The reason this type of price discrepancy sometimes occurs is that airlines want to put your entire group into a single fare bucket. In this case, there were only two tickets left in the $117 fare bucket, with plenty more in the $178 bucket. Searching for three tickets priced all three at $178, whereas searching for two priced them at $117 (and I knew I could book the third ticket for $178).

Precisely how much cheaper an OTA would have to be in order to book there is entirely dependent on how much value you place on the three factors above. If you're someone whose plans are constantly changing, you'd place a higher value on the ability to easily shift your itinerary. If money's tight and $100 could mean the difference between taking a trip or not, getting the cheapest price possible is what's important.

Unless it's a mistake fare—when an airline erroneously sells a flight at an unbelievably low price (more on these in Chapter 12)—I personally value booking directly at about $25. If I find a ticket I can book directly from United for $300, that same flight would need to be under $275 on an OTA for me to consider straying.

If it's a mistake fare situation, in which issuing tickets quickly is paramount and the 24-hour rule can give you some room to make a final decision, booking directly is far more important to me, and it's something I'd personally value at closer to $200.

Let's take two examples.

Rachel just got an alert for a Delta mistake fare from Chicago to Tokyo for just $230 roundtrip. Booking on an OTA, though, she can get the price down to $210. Where should Rachel book?

Verdict: Rachel would do herself a favor to book directly with Delta because mistake fares can disappear in an instant. If she purchases on an OTA but her ticket hasn't been issued by the time Delta fixes the mistake, it's highly unlikely she would receive the ticket at the mistake price. (To be clear, you can't be charged a higher price without your consent, they just won't issue you the ticket.) Booking directly means the ticket gets issued near instantaneously, and it gives her protection to cancel fee-free within 24 hours if she changes her mind.

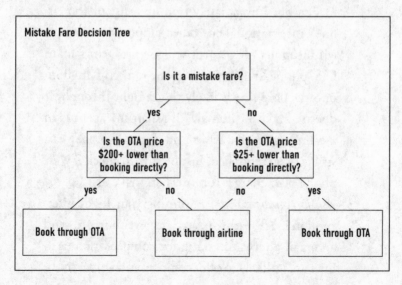

WHAT TO DO WHEN A FLIGHT GETS DELAYED
OR CANCELED

Three things you should always do if your flight gets delayed or canceled:

1. *Do your own research*: If you need to get rebooked on a new flight, rather than waiting to hear what rebooking options they present you, check the airline's (or airline partners') flight schedule to see what other possibilities would work best for your situation. You're always your own best advocate.

2. *Call international customer support*: When a flight gets canceled, airline agents have hundreds of people to rebook, and even more when multiple flights are impacted by bad weather. Rather than spending hours in line, what I'll do is get in line but immediately pull up a list of the airline's international customer support numbers. A Minneapolis snowstorm will tie up Delta's main U.S. phone line, but calling the United Kingdom or Singapore line is likely to get right through. It doesn't make a difference if an airline agent is in a call center halfway around the world; they can still get you rebooked. Just be sure to check if your phone plan charges for international calls.

3. *Ask for compensation*: Assuming your flight interruption isn't weather-related, it never hurts to send an email afterward asking for compensation. Airlines are unlikely to offer compensation proactively,

but if you follow up after a big delay and politely explain why it was a hardship, you'll almost always be given hundreds of dollars or thousands of frequent flyer miles for your trouble. (This is especially true on European flights, where regulation EU261 requires airlines to compensate passengers for long delays and cancellations.)

Monica, meanwhile, found a $500 roundtrip flight on Google Flights from Boston to Rome this November. When she checked the same route and dates on Skyscanner, the price dropped to $350 on Vayama, a smaller OTA. Where should Monica book?

Verdict: This is not a mistake fare like Rachel's, so there's less worry the deal will disappear any minute. As a result, the ticket-issuing speed and 24-hour rule protections are less important. Is $150 worth some level of extra hassle in the unlikely event Monica needs to change her itinerary? For most of us, the answer is probably yes, in which case booking the $350 Vayama fare is the way to go.

With all those considerations in mind, buying flights where you're most comfortable on a personal level is the best strategy. If that means booking directly, great; if that means saving every possible penny, swell. Vacations, like the flight-booking process, are best when they take stress away rather than add it.

WHICH AIRPORTS GET THE MOST (AND FEWEST) CHEAP FLIGHTS?

I grew up in rural Ohio, in a place that wasn't even large enough to be classified as a town (technically it was a village). The idea of getting affordable flights out of my home airport, Dayton—much less cheap ones—was inconceivable.

That may have been true when I was a teenager, but nowadays we're living in the Golden Age of Cheap Flights. In the past few years, we've seen roundtrip flights from Dayton as low as $294 to Germany or Austria, $640 to Australia, and $555 to Singapore. Far from being reserved exclusively for big cities, cheap flights are everywhere now.

And yet, our collective understanding of airfare hasn't caught up. Many people still believe that even if good fares occasionally pop up, they only do so in New York City or Los Angeles. *Cheap flights are great, but they don't happen in small airports, right?*

This pessimism leads to some unfortunate outcomes. When I travel home and hear about the $1,000+ fares my Ohio friends paid to visit Europe (in 2019!), I'm left in horror. To paraphrase Michael Gerson, they're falling victim to the soft insidiousness of low expectations.

There are two principal factors in determining how many cheap flights a given city will have: population and competition. Without a doubt, large cities get the *most* deals. In 2019, the top five cities for cheap flights by quantity were New York, Los Angeles, Boston, San Francisco, and Chicago.

However, not every large city gets the same number of deals. The five cities above aren't just large; they also see a ton of competition among airlines, and as we discussed in Chapter 6, that competition drives down fares.

There are some large cities that are hindered by one airline holding a monopoly on flights, tamping down competition and limiting the number of fare sales. Take Houston. It's the fourth-largest city in the United States by population, but in 2019 its primary airport, IAH, was just sixteenth in cheap flight quantity. The reason: United Airlines. Like Atlanta for Delta and Dallas for American, Houston is a hub for United, and that carrier has a monopoly on the airport's flights.

Though monopolized cities have fewer cheap flights than expected for their size, they're not completely barren. They still get dozens of bona fide cheap flights each month. Plus, like we learned in Chapter 7, hub cities are often the beneficiary of fare wars. While an airline monopoly prevents Houston residents from getting a significantly higher number of deals, that monopoly also opens the door for competitors to come in with cheap fares of their own. In fact, if you live in an airport controlled by one airline, the best deals are usually on their competitors.

Smaller cities, meanwhile, tend to have fewer airlines and fewer flights, which leads to generally higher fares. Although smaller airports don't get the most deals, that's a far cry from getting none. Living in Omaha doesn't mean resigning yourself to moral victories, feeling good paying $900 for a flight to Rome because it's less than the $1,000 your friend paid.

Despite lower quantity, I would argue that people living near small airports in fact get the *best* deals. To understand why, we have to consider normal prices.

Flights from New York City—the cheap flight capital of America by volume—to Europe are normally around $700 roundtrip these days. (Note that this figure is a very loose average of how much one could generally expect to pay for the route. Specific fares vary significantly according to when they were booked, date of travel, routing, sheer luck, and dozens of other factors.) Flights from Omaha to Europe, meanwhile, are normally closer to $1,500 roundtrip.

When a cheap flight pops up from Omaha to Europe, like the $304 roundtrip Omaha–Munich fare that dropped in August 2019, Nebraskans who got the deal saved $1,200 off normal prices. In order for New Yorkers to save $1,200 on flights to Europe, the airline would have to give them a free ticket *plus* $500 straight cash homie.

But Scott, why would an airline drop its fares from Omaha to Europe all the way down to $300?

As special as Omaha is, typically what's happening is the airline is running a regional or nationwide sale that happens to include Omaha and many other airports, big and small. For example, those $304 fares to Munich weren't just available out of Omaha but 120 U.S. cities in total, from Albany to Yuma. Though fares that good aren't common, they're not rare either. Virtually every month for the past five years there's been a Big Europe Sale (as we discussed in Chapter 7), helping people in less populated areas get the types of cheap flights more commonly found in big cities.

Just as New York sees more cheap flights than Omaha, so too are there some destinations that see more cheap flights than others. It's not entirely random. Rather, it follows many of the same principles, including size and competition, as well as flight scheduling and other business factors.

Here are some of the international destinations most likely to see flights from the United States under $500 roundtrip:

- **North America**: Domestic flights, as well as those to Mexico and Canada, have the cheapest fares on average.
- **Caribbean**: Some islands like Puerto Rico, Aruba,

Curaçao, and Turks and Caicos regularly see cheap flights from the mainland United States. Others, like Jamaica, Grenada, and the British Virgin Islands, rarely see cheap fares, except if you're departing from Florida.

- **Central America**: Costa Rica is the real belle of the ball here, followed by Guatemala and Panama.
- **Northern South America**: Colombia, Ecuador, and Peru have become remarkably affordable in the past few years. Fares to Colombia used to typically exceed $600, but nowadays they regularly drop under $300 roundtrip. All three countries are tourist favorites, and they're close enough (unlike southern South America) for planes to run efficient schedules with there-and-back flights on the same day.
- **Western Europe**: The most common cities for cheap flights are generally large ones with high tourism demand: Paris, Rome, Amsterdam, Barcelona, Madrid, Reykjavík, and, to a lesser extent, London. Some other cities will have stretches when cheap fares constantly pop up—Dublin, Copenhagen, Zurich, parts of Germany—but these are less frequent.
- **China**: In part because of competition from burgeoning Chinese airlines and in part due to corporate travelers clamoring for business class seats, flights to China are typically cheaper than flights to Jamaica or other nearby destinations.

On the other end of the spectrum, these are the international destinations that are least likely to see cheap flights from the United States:

- **Africa**: There's a combination of factors working against cheap flights to Africa: lower demand from tourists, less competition among airlines, and long distances to fly. The good news is that fares have recently been trending cheaper and cheaper, especially as more airlines start nonstop routes from the United States. Though not yet under $500, we're already starting to see fares under $650 somewhat regularly, a far cry from a few years ago when anything below $1,000 was a rarity. The cheapest countries are typically Morocco, South Africa, Kenya, Tanzania, and Uganda.

- **Oceania**: Though a highly sought-after tourist destination, the distance is a major hindrance for cheap flight availability. Fares should continue to improve as more fuel-efficient planes enter the market, but until a budget airline enters the U.S.–Oceania market, it's unlikely to see this route drop below $500 consistently. The cheapest destinations are usually Australia, New Zealand, the Cook Islands, and Tahiti.

- **The Middle East and Central Asia**: Long distance and middling tourism demand keep fares relatively high on these routes. Israel and Jordan are most likely to see cheap fares from the United States.

- **Southern South America**: These flights are expensive because of a weird scheduling quirk. When a plane from the United States arrives in southern South America, the airline typically lets the plane sit on the ground until the evening, when it flies back. The reasoning is a bit complex, but in short it's because flights take ten or more hours and there's no time zone change, like there is with flights to Europe, so a quick turnaround would bring passengers back to the United States late at night, past when they'd be able to catch connecting flights. Airlines want to keep their planes in the sky as much as possible in order to maximize revenue, so they view flights to southern South America as an inefficient use of planes. Fewer flights means limited competition and increased fares. Still, there are some glimmers of hope, especially for Brazil, where a number of new airlines have entered the market and helped drive down fares.

If you have your heart set on visiting a not-often-cheap destination, don't give up hope. Even though you should temper expectations a bit and not expect to see $300 fares, neither should you just accept that $2,000 fares are okay. Though it may require some creativity (like Shanna Lathwell driving her family to Chicago in Chapter 4) and some patience (sub-$600 flights to Bali pop up only a few times a year), nowadays, in the Golden Age of Cheap Flights, you can fly from the United States to virtually anywhere in the world for under $800 roundtrip.

WHAT ABOUT BUDGET AIRLINES AND BASIC ECONOMY?

One of the most heated topics at cheap flight bacchanals is whether basic economy is Actually Good or Actually Bad.

In one corner we have a debauched clan throwing verbal haymakers about the indignity of being nickel-and-dimed. It's like there's a fee for everything! Sure, the flight may seem cheap, but that's just a bait-and-switch once you account for all the up-charges. What's next, a fee to use the bathroom?

In the other corner, we have a carousing caravan of travelers who love cheap flights and hate paying for things they don't use. You'd be annoyed if your restaurant bill charged you for a slice of pie you never ordered; why wouldn't you be similarly annoyed if your ticket price is inflated to include a checked bag that you never use? Optionality is a beautiful thing. Pay for what you value and save money on what you don't.

Before we take sides in the Great Basic Economy Debate, let's step back and understand how we got here: a decades-long war between full-service airlines and budget airlines.

Remember, for the first half century or so of commercial aviation, flying was so expensive that only the wealthy could afford tickets. After World War II, airlines and the government wanted to build up the civil aviation industry and encourage people to fly, but the public was reluctant. The solution: make flying as luxurious as possible to overcome the public's fear of this new and dangerous mode of transportation. Flight attendants, bougie meals and drinks, roomy seats—everything was included in the ticket.

Around the time deregulation arrived in the late 1970s and cheaper fares made flying more accessible to the general public, Southwest Airlines helped kick off the budget airline revolution. Whereas full-service airlines included standard amenities—meals, seat reservations, a first class cabin—Southwest tried apply to optional fees like checked bags or reserved seats. Un-bundled fares lower the airlines' tax bills.

When Southwest launched, it was clear what a budget air-line was: fewer amenities and cheaper fares. They flew shorter routes, and their planes had no premium cabin seating or elabo-rate onboard meals. Full-service airlines, meanwhile, had exten-sive route networks, long-haul flights, first class cabins, and fine dining on board.

Nowadays, the line between what's a budget airline (also known as "low-cost carriers" or "ultra-low-cost carriers") and what's a full-service airline (also known as "legacy airlines") is getting increasingly blurred. What precisely is the difference these days?

What Are Budget Airlines?

Consider this mental exercise: Which of these airlines would you consider a budget carrier, and which would you consider a full-service airline?

Airline A: The cheapest fares include two checked bags and two carry-ons, families with kids are seated together, and there are no fees to change or cancel a reservation.

Airline B: The cheapest fares include no checked bags, full-size carry-ons are not permitted, family seating and advanced seat selection are not available, and tickets cannot be changed or canceled, even for a fee.

Airline A is Southwest Airlines, a "budget" airline. Air-line B is United Airlines, one of the oldest "full-service" airlines.

something new: none of that. They made the entire airplane an economy cabin, stripped out the free meals and champagne, and charged way less for tickets.

This new model was a huge hit. Over the next few decades, as flying became increasingly safe and affordable, price became the most important differentiator for the mass public. Southwest and other budget airlines grew exponentially by focusing on being the cheapest option. Meanwhile, many of the seemingly invincible full-service airlines like TWA and Pan Am, who were focused on being the swankiest, fell.

Tired of getting clobbered on price by budget airlines, full-service carriers tried a new tactic: creating their own budget subsidiary airlines. Delta created Song Airlines, United created Ted Airlines, Air France created Joon. All were intended to be budget options controlled by larger airlines, and all were miserable failures that folded within a few years.

Finally, after years of budget airlines growing faster and more profitably than the rest of the industry, full-service airlines figured out a way to take on budget airlines: unbundling. Rather than sell expensive tickets with tons of amenities automatically included, they would sell cheaper tickets and charge extra for extras. In 2008 full-service airlines began charging for checked bags, and around 2016 they unveiled basic economy fares. These would allow full-service airlines to compete on price with budget airlines—Delta called them "Spirit [Airlines]–match fares"—but to do so with the advantage of their existing route network and infrastructure.

Another factor pushing full-service airlines to unbundle: the tax code. The 7.5 percent federal excise tax on airfare doesn't

Now that full-service airlines offer basic economy tickets, in a way, all airlines have become budget airlines. When all of United's fares were bundled, it made sense to distinguish them from a budget airline like Spirit, whose fares didn't include amenities. But nowadays, in an age when virtually all airlines have a lengthy menu of add-on fees, labeling arguments are fussy and meaningless. The term "budget airline" can be misleading when it prompts you to make an assumption about the service being offered. There's not a lot left to distinguish a full-service carrier from a budget carrier.

What's more, airlines evolve over time. JetBlue was founded as a budget airline, but it repositioned as it grew. Now its amenities exceed most full-service airlines, complete with satellite TV, a first class cabin, above-average legroom, and free snacks. Frontier went the opposite direction, beginning as more of a full-service airline before transforming into a budget carrier.

IS _____ AIRLINE SAFE?

The U.S. government doesn't allow just any airline to fly within its national borders. Only airlines from countries that have received a passing grade from the Federal Aviation Administration are permitted to fly to the United States. The FAA uses criteria set forth by the United Nations, evaluating a country's aviation authority on measures like safety protocols, oversight, and training.

Even if you're traveling abroad on an airline you've never heard of, flying is still one of the safest ways to get around. According to the National Safety Council, the lifetime odds of dying in a plane accident are approximately 1 in 10,000, and you have even better odds if you fly only commercial, rather than private, aircraft. By comparison, fatality odds are higher if you're driving (1 in 114), biking (1 in 4,486), and even walking (1 in 647). Still, I understand the worry; even after years of flying I get a knotted stomach during turbulence. If that's you too, next time you're in a rough patch, do what I do: Look over to a flight attendant and admire, even in choppy air, the look of utter boredom on their face. It always calms me down.

One distinguishing factor to be aware of: Business travelers rarely fly on budget airlines like Spirit. This is for a number of reasons. First, many large companies have corporate contracts for discounted rates with full-service airlines. Second, business travelers themselves often prefer full-service airlines because they have more generous rewards programs and business class cabins into which, even if they're not ticketed, they can often secure an upgrade via elite status. Budget airlines, meanwhile, target leisure travelers as their core audience. Their fares tend to be lower (vacationers are more price-sensitive than business travelers), and they're more likely to have last-minute deals because they have fewer late-booking business travelers to gouge.

The Hidden Reason I Avoid Budget Airlines

Before I explain why I typically avoid budget airlines, I do want to offer a bit of praise. The fact that we're currently living in the Golden Age of Cheap Flights is in large part thanks to them. Budget airlines and their substantially lower fares have forced full-service carriers to respond by slashing their own fares, because they know that travelers value a cheap fare more than staying loyal to a single airline. The $300 roundtrip flights to Europe that we see today would not have happened in a world without competition from budget airlines. Even if you never fly one, cheap flight aficionados owe a debt of gratitude to budget airlines and the downward pressure they put on airfare industry-wide.

That said, when I take a trip, I usually steer away from budget airlines. It's not because of fees or frequent flyer miles. Instead, it's because of the potential of a trip-shattering delay.

Let's say our two travelers from earlier, Priya and Tom, have moved to New York City and are looking for flights to Rome leaving on November 15 and returning on November 22. At time of writing, the two best fares are $400 for nonstop flights on Norwegian Airlines (a budget carrier) or $465 for nonstop flights on Delta (a full-service airline).

Priya bought the $465 Delta flight, while Tom went for the $400 Norwegian one. As luck would have it, the morning of November 15, both got alerts that their flights were canceled for mechanical issues. They called up their respective airline's customer service agents, desperate for another way to get to Rome.

The Delta agent told Priya she had a ton of options. She could get a seat on Delta-partner Alitalia, either their nonstop flight leaving a few hours earlier than her original itinerary or a night flight leaving a few hours later. Alternatively, she could catch the Delta flight to Amsterdam and then the KLM flight onward to Rome, or the Delta flight to Boston paired with an Alitalia flight to Rome. There were at least a dozen other partner options that made her head spin, all of which would get her to Italy within a few hours of her original flight. She settled on the first nonstop Alitalia flight.

Tom was not so fortunate. He called Norwegian, hoping to have a slate of alternative flights from which to choose. No dice. Like most budget airlines, Norwegian rarely partners with other carriers. In addition, it has almost no interline agreements, when two airlines agree to carry one another's passengers, especially in case of delays or cancellations. Instead, Tom would have to wait for the next Norwegian flight to Rome. He asked if he could leave later that night, only to discover the next Norwegian flight out was 2 days away, shaving his already-brief 7-day vacation down to 5. With no good alternatives, he grudgingly accepted the new flight.

This is why I try to avoid budget airlines: When things go wrong, they can go really wrong. Full-service airlines have extensive, redundant schedules and large partner networks. If your flight gets significantly delayed or canceled, there's usually a wealth of alternatives. Even beyond partner networks, most full-service airlines have interline agreements with one another. For example, even though United and Delta are competitors, not partners, if a United flight gets canceled, they have an interline agreement with Delta whereby they can get stranded United passengers onto a Delta flight if needed.

Budget airlines rarely have such interline agreements, and they have few (and sometimes no) partner airlines either. If your budget airline's flight gets canceled, typically your only options are finding another flight on that airline or a refund. Finding an alternative flight wouldn't be so bad if the airline had hundreds of planes flying thousands of routes every day, but many budget airlines fly a given route only a few times per week. Delta and their partners currently operate 19 flights a week between JFK and Rome (and hundreds more options if you account for connecting flights), while Norwegian has just 5 flights a week on that route. What's more, using Tom's example, even if there were a seat available on Norwegian's Boston–Rome flight, because the airline has no partners and doesn't fly New York–Boston, they would have no way to get him up to Massachusetts for the alternative flight.

As a slight caveat, it's important to bear in mind that flight cancellations are quite rare. In September 2019, just 0.7 percent of Norwegian's flights were canceled. If a budget airline is $500 cheaper than the next best alternative, I'm going to buy that ticket and pocket that $500. But if it's a savings of only $25 or $50, I'll generally opt for a full-service airline. Though highly unlikely, the downside risk is too catastrophic to ignore completely.

What Is Basic Economy?

Before debating its merits, let's explore what makes a ticket basic economy. In short, basic economy is a fare that has fewer amenities included than main economy. It's not always called basic economy; sometimes airlines brand it as Saver or Light or something similar. The specific restrictions vary by airline and route, but generally speaking, basic economy ticket holders:

- Cannot change or cancel their tickets (even for a fee)
- Don't get a free checked bag
- Aren't eligible for complimentary upgrades or other elite perks
- Board the plane last
- Don't get free advance seat selection
- Still get a free full-size carry-on

There are some notable exceptions. For instance, Alaska Airlines allows basic economy ticket holders to choose their seat in advance, while United bars domestic basic economy flyers from carrying on a full-size bag. American bars their basic economy passengers from making changes to their tickets if they're flying within the Western Hemisphere but allows them to make changes if they're flying to Europe. Because the specific contours of basic economy vary widely depending on who you're flying and where you're going, make sure to read the fine print in advance. (Also note that, at time of writing, basic economy isn't an option on flights from the United States to Asia, Africa, or Australia; the cheapest fares are main economy.)

There are a few ways to get around basic economy restrictions. If you want just one specific amenity (say, early seat selection), airlines will often let basic economy flyers purchase it à la carte. If you want multiple items (say, early seat selection and early boarding), you can always book in main economy, though you may have to do so when you purchase your ticket. The price difference between basic economy and main economy is highly variable. I've seen it as cheap as $5 and as high as $200, though generally it's in the range of $30 to $60 each way.

THREE COST-EFFICIENT WAYS TO GET
BUSINESS CLASS SEATS

Business class flights are *expensive*, especially on international flights when they're most coveted. Long-haul business class flights are usually at least 4–5 times more expensive than economy, and sometimes 8–10 times more. For instance, at time of writing you could book a British Airways flight from New York City to Paris for $297 roundtrip. A business class seat on that flight, meanwhile, is going for $3,008 roundtrip. While we'd all love a more comfortable ride across the ocean, it's important to ask yourself (earnestly!): Would you rather take 1 luxurious flight or 10 regular flights?

If you're truly keen on getting business class seats, here are the most cost-efficient ways:

- *Use miles*: It takes time and energy to get good at the miles and points game, but for those of us who can't afford $3,000 tickets, it's the most accessible way to sit at the front of the plane.
- *Get bumped*: Next time a flight you're on is oversold and you've got flexible plans, ask to get bumped up to business class on your new flight. It won't work every time, but if there's room and the airline is desperate, they'll gladly accommodate you in return for your giving up your original seat.
- *Bid for upgrades*: Airlines are increasingly selling empty business class seats at check-in to the highest bidder. Though they will still be considerably

more expensive than coach, paid upgrade bids are almost always quite a bit cheaper than normal business class prices.

It's also important not to assume upgrading to main economy gets you all the perks. If you're flying domestically, upgrading to main economy likely won't get you a free checked bag, for instance. Check the fine print.

Another option for mitigating basic economy's restrictions is an airline credit card. These cards bypass some of the most onerous aspects of basic economy, typically entitling the cardholder to perks like a free checked bag (often for everyone on the itinerary) and early boarding. (Note that most airline credit cards do not include early seat selection as a perk.) On some airlines, you have to use the airline credit card to buy the tickets in order to get the benefits, while on others the perk is tied to your frequent flyer number and you can pay for the ticket however you like. Either way, I'd recommend bringing the card to the airport.

Is Basic Economy Bad?

Depends on whom you ask.

If you travel light and prize cheap flights above all else, basic economy is great. Why pay for a checked bag if you never bring one? Similarly, if you have an airline credit card that already gets you a free bag, it pairs perfectly with a cheap fare that doesn't include luggage.

For others, basic economy can be frustrating, even feeling

like an affront. After all, if you need to check a bag on your flight to Europe and don't have an airline credit card, basic economy restrictions could mean you're no longer getting the cheapest flight. And if you're traveling with a group, you now have to pay for the "privilege" of sitting together. Imagine if a restaurant required customers to pay a fee in order to be seated at the same table. Our outrage is perhaps less about the fee than the audacity.

People have a well-attuned bullshit meter these days, and rightly so. Any time I talk to someone about cheap flights I've seen lately, the first question is invariably "What about the fees?" They're not wrong. Booking a "cheap" flight with unavoidable fees means it was a bait-and-switch, not a cheap flight.

It all boils down to where you think the default ought to be set. What should be included with your ticket and what should cost extra? Airlines *could* include lobster dinners with your ticket like the old days, but even basic economy's haters would be upset if this meant flights were now twice as expensive. On the other side, airlines *could* charge passengers a fee to use the bathroom, but that would outrage even basic economy's defenders.

Put another way, are basic economy's fees truly optional? Can you reasonably travel on a basic economy fare, or is it just a sneaky way for airlines to charge more?

If you always check a bag and need early seat selection, those basic economy fees feel oppressive, not optional. Conversely, if you travel only with a carry-on bag and don't care where you sit, you may be glad to not have to pay for perks you don't care about. Though there's no objectively correct answer, I have a prediction: Once the novelty of basic economy wears off, few would propose going back to more expensive bundled fares.

Much of our angst may be traced to the newness of basic economy. In 2008, when full-service airlines first began charging passengers for checked bags, the public was livid. According to an IBM survey, 78 percent said that baggage fees are "rip-offs." Hotels would offer to reimburse guests who showed receipts for bag fees, and entire companies popped up promising to ship bags cheaper than what the airlines charged. Bag fees felt wrong and unnatural in part because they were novel. More than a decade later, though, we've gotten used to being charged for luggage. It's become banal. "Back in my day we used to get free checked bags" feels like something an old-timer might say.

The same process is likely playing out with basic economy. It's new and scary. There's a strong and understandable backlash to being charged for things that used to be complimentary. But with time, that memory will fade and basic economy will become normalized. Our kids will one day ask us if it's true that you could buy a ticket that automatically included checked baggage and early seat selection.

For now, the good news is that the Golden Age of Cheap Flights is happening across the board, not just in basic economy. Many of us bristle at the add-on fees, but we're not stuck choosing between cheap flights *or* main economy. Though $300 basic economy flights to Europe may be a nonstarter for some, is $400 for main economy so bad?

HOW CAN I AVOID FEES?

Before it went out of business, WOW Air used to grab headlines all the time with promises of "$99 fares to Europe!" (Never mind that $99 was the one-way price; for people who'd like to return home, the return fare was typically at least an additional $200.)

I heard from some travelers who booked $300 WOW flights to Europe. They were thrilled with the fare, until they read the fine print. In their excitement, they'd assumed that even if they had to pay bag fees, it would be a standard $30 each way. No big deal.

To their surprise, they found out that WOW didn't limit their fees to checked baggage like most airlines; they charged for carry-ons larger than a purse as well. And the fee wasn't $30 each way, it was $65. Nor was it the standard practice where passengers are charged once on the outbound and once on the return. Instead, the carry-on fee was assessed on each leg of the flight. All WOW flights connected in Iceland en route to mainland Europe, so a $300 flight from the United States to Paris could carry an additional $260 in fees *just for a carry-on*.

Most airline's fees aren't nearly as egregious or unavoidable, but that doesn't mean they're not loathsome all the same. They can turn what you thought was a great deal into an expensive one.

GET GLOBAL ENTRY, NOT TSA PRECHECK

If you're thinking about getting TSA PreCheck to speed through airport security lines (You should! It's great!), opt for Global Entry instead. Global Entry—which lets you skip the normal immigration and customs lines when you get back from a trip abroad—only costs $15 more, and it includes TSA PreCheck.

A few overarching rules to bear in mind before we discuss specific categories of fees:

First, assume nothing. If you assume that your United basic economy ticket to San Diego includes a full-size carry-on or that upgrading to main economy includes a checked bag, you're going to have a bad time. Always read the fine print. You don't want to wind up with a $300 flight to Europe that charges an additional $260 for a carry-on bag.

Second, not all basic economy flights are the same. For example, basic economy tickets on Delta don't include seat selection, while basic economy tickets on Alaska do. Even within the same airline, basic economy can vary by route. United basic economy fares don't include a full-size carry-on for domestic flights, but they do include one on flights to Europe.

Third, on many airlines, it can be cheaper to prepay for optional items. On Spirit Airlines, for instance, a full-size carry-on bag can range in price from $35 during booking to $45 during check-in to $55 at the ticketing desk to $65 at the gate. Spirit makes a substantial profit on its passengers not reading the fine print.

Last, if you're considering a basic economy fare but want to check a bag and/or reserve seats in advance, it might be cheaper to upgrade to main economy. For example, on TAP Air Portugal flights between the United States and Europe, adding a checked bag to a basic economy fare usually costs $92 each way (yikes!) while upgrading to a main economy fare that includes a checked bag is typically around $35 each way. The price to upgrade from basic to main varies across routes and airlines, so it won't always be cheaper to bundle, but it's always worth checking.

With those precepts in mind, these are the three most common fees that plague flyers, and how to avoid them.

Bag Fees

Nowadays, the cheapest fares almost never include checked baggage, even on international flights. Upgrading from basic to main economy won't get you a free checked bag if you're flying domestically or to Latin America or the Caribbean. A checked bag can cost anywhere from $10 on short flights to $100 on certain long-haul routes. (Southwest is currently the lone holdout that still doesn't charge bag fees: something worth accounting for when comparing prices if you're planning on checking luggage.)

There are a few strategies for avoiding checked-bag fees. The first is so self-explanatory that it hardly bears mentioning, but the easiest way to avoid paying for checked bags is to avoid checking a bag, whether by packing light or stuffing your carry-on. Whenever I travel overseas, I pack no more than a week's worth of clothes in my Tortuga backpack. It fits fine, it's not too heavy, and if I'm going to be traveling longer than a week, I'll plan to do laundry. The key is picking a bag that's large enough to fit a week's worth of clothes but small enough to fit in an overhead bin.

Most airlines still allow each passenger to bring one full-size carry-on (think a large backpack or roller suitcase), regardless of the fare they've booked. However, there are a few notable exceptions, including most budget airlines (Frontier charges $37 to $60, depending on when you purchase, and Spirit, as mentioned earlier) and United for basic economy flights domestically and within most of the Western Hemisphere.

The simplest way to get free checked baggage is to open an airline's credit card. Across the board these cards include the perk of a free checked bag anytime you're flying that airline. Even more, the free checked-bag allowance applies to your travel companions as well. If a family of four each wanted to check a bag on their domestic American flight, American's credit card would save them $60 apiece roundtrip, $240 in total.

There's another possibility if you have young kids. Even basic economy fares include a free checked car seat, and you can get a simple large travel bag for the car seat, large enough to include space for another bag where the child would sit.

If your motivation to check a bag is just so you don't have to lug it around the airport, you've got another option. During check-in, take a look at the seat map and see how full the flight seems. If it's nearly sold out, there won't be enough room for everyone's carry-on bags and chances are the gate agent will ask for volunteers to check their bag to their final destination, free of charge.

Advance Seat Selection Fees

The newest fee is charging passengers to choose their seats in advance. Airlines have realized that many passengers are willing to pay extra to avoid the dreaded middle seat when traveling solo, or to sit together when traveling with companions. (Unfortunately, most airline credit cards don't include early seat selection on basic economy fares as a perk.)

One way to make sure you're sitting with your travel companions is to fly Southwest. They use an open seating plan, and travelers are permitted on board by order of when they checked in (aside from those with elite status or who paid to jump the line). Set yourself a calendar reminder to check in exactly 24 hours ahead of your flight and you'll be certain to sit with your travel companions. If you're traveling with young children, you'll get to board early regardless.

But if you're traveling on an airline that does charge for advance seat selection, it can sometimes be a better value to switch from basic to main economy. Let's consider a United flight from Boston to London. If you buy a basic economy fare, advance seat selection starts out at $15 and checking a bag is $70. Meanwhile, buying up to main economy—which includes advance seat selection and a checked bag—is just $65. If you want multiple amenities, it's often a better deal to upgrade rather than pay à la carte. (As always, be sure to read the fine print; main economy includes a checked bag on international flights but *not* on domestic flights, for instance.)

Assuming you're sticking with basic economy, check when your airline allows basic economy passengers to start selecting seats. For some it'll be as much as a week in advance of travel, though 24 hours is more typical. Set yourself a calendar reminder to book seats as soon as they open up in order to beat out less diligent flyers.

Here's another trick to get a good seat in basic economy from travel blogger Derek Earl Baron. When you check in for a flight, as a basic economy passenger you'll often be shown just a few available seats from which to choose. Lest you think you have to select one right away, you don't. Instead, refresh the seat selection page every few minutes. The seats you can choose from will usually change as other passengers check in and make their selections. Keep doing this until a good window or aisle seat becomes available for you to snag. Although this trick doesn't work for every airline, it's an easy loophole on those it does.

If traveling with a young child, ask the gate agent if you can be seated next to one another. Most will oblige because they want to keep families together, and most passengers you switch with will be grateful to avoid sitting next to a crying baby.

If you're just traveling with other adults and you aren't seated together, though, your last resort is old-school: Ask a neighbor if they'll switch after boarding. People may be reluctant to give up an aisle seat for a middle one or to move back in the plane, but if you're offering them a better seat, many travelers are glad to trade.

Cancellation Fees

Most airlines charge a minimum of $200—and significantly more if it's an international flight—to cancel a ticket and refund the remainder. And that's assuming you haven't purchased a basic economy fare, which on most airlines is completely nonrefundable. (For our purposes, let's assume in this section that you haven't bought an exorbitantly expensive refundable ticket.)

Aside from booking on Southwest Airlines (the one airline that doesn't charge fees to cancel a ticket, and instead lets you retain the full value in travel credit), there are a handful of ways to alter your reservation, even if you've booked a basic economy fare. First, remember our trusty old friend, the 24-hour rule? As long as you booked directly with the airline, by federal law you have a 24-hour grace period after purchase to cancel your ticket without any penalty.

If it's been more than 24 hours, there are only a few scenarios that would allow you to cancel without a penalty (or get a refund at all with a basic economy fare). The first is if there are extenuating personal circumstances, things like a medical emergency or jury duty; in those cases, airlines will typically relax their normal fees. Same goes if there's a natural disaster or other major event.

The more likely (though still improbable) savior if you're stuck with a flight you don't want is a schedule change. I once booked a flight home to Dayton that got me in late on Christmas Eve. Not exactly ideal, but it was the most affordable option. A few weeks after booking, the airline emailed me that my flight time had changed, and it included a note to call them if this caused a problem. Never mind that the change was just two minutes—this was my chance. I called and said that, while the new flight times would indeed be problematic, I'd found a flight the day before with tickets still available. Could I be switched to that flight? A few minutes later, I was the proud owner of a December 23 ticket, having to pay neither a change fee nor the extortionary price those flights sold for.

Do be aware that schedule change policies vary by airline and most require shifts of at least one to two hours to be eligible for a refund. There's flexibility around these rules, though, as evidenced by my two-minute schedule change.

There was some good news in 2020 when most US airlines announced they were gutting change fees. While a step in the right direction, many exceptions remain. First, at time of writing, most airlines don't allow changes at all—free or otherwise—

on basic economy tickets. Second, there are still change fees on many long-haul international flights. Third, even on tickets where change fees are gone, you still have to pay up if the new flight is more expensive. And lastly, if the new flight is cheaper, not all airlines will let you keep the fare difference.

Some people buy trip insurance, but once again, knowing the fine print is crucial. Trip insurance typically provides reimbursement for only the types of extenuating circumstances that airlines or credit cards already cover, like a medical emergency. You're rarely able to get a refund if you simply decide to not take a trip because you changed your mind.

One thing not to do is take an ignorance-is-bliss approach to fees. Years ago, I was in Europe and booked a Ryanair flight. With the chutzpah of youth, I figured there was no need to read through Ryanair's fee page. After all, I only had a small bag and didn't care what seat I got. What could go wrong? Turns out, Ryanair had a policy requiring passengers to print their boarding pass before arriving at the airport. The fee to check in at the airport: $90, over twice the cost of my flight. Livid as I was, I learned an expensive lesson.

Ignoring add-on fees won't change the fact that they exist, small booby traps that threaten your trip. Being mindful of the fine print and making a plan to avoid getting hit is the key to ensuring that fees don't eat away at what had been a great flight deal.

THE ONE AIRLINE THAT'S DIFFERENT

Over the past decade, as the aviation industry has shifted toward unbundled tickets—offering low base fares but charging passengers for optional items like seat selection and checked bags—one airline has consistently bucked the trend: Southwest Airlines.

Southwest, the category-bending carrier that flew more domestic passengers in 2018 than any other carrier in the United States, operates quite a bit differently than almost all other airlines. It often gets referred to as a budget airline, but as we discussed, this label is equal parts correct and wildly misleading. If "budget airline" means a carrier that doesn't have a business class or isn't part of an alliance like Oneworld, then Southwest indeed qualifies. If instead "budget airline" means a carrier that tacks on tons of fees for checked bags and the like, by that definition Southwest is the only *nonbudget airline* in the United States.

Because Southwest operates differently than other airlines, it presents an opportunity for travelers in certain situations to save significant amounts of money. Before exploring those scenarios, though, it's helpful to first familiarize ourselves with what makes Southwest unique.

Free checked bags: Over a decade since U.S. airlines began charging extra for checked bags, Southwest is the only carrier that still currently includes two free checked bags with every ticket, in addition to two carry-on items.

Free changes/cancellations: On most airlines, you cannot change the ticket at all if you've booked a basic economy fare. Southwest, meanwhile, doesn't charge any fees to change flights, even on their cheapest tickets. Nor do they charge any fees to cancel a booking, so long as you cancel at least ten minutes before the flight departs. If you paid with points, they get redeposited in your account. If you paid with a credit card, you get a full refund in Southwest travel credit that has to be used within the next twelve months.

Sit together free: More and more airlines are charging a fee for advance seat selection, which many families grudgingly pay in order to sit together. Southwest (which does first-come first-served seating rather than preassigning seats) lets families with young children board before most passengers, allowing them to sit together without paying extra for the privilege. Even if your travel companions don't include small children, you can still sit together by setting yourself an alarm to check in exactly 24 hours before the flight so you're assigned an early boarding number.

The fact that Southwest eschews fees isn't just beneficial for travelers who hate feeling nickel-and-dimed. It also gives you a chance to be opportunistic in a number of different scenarios.

Take my friend Miguel for example. He wanted to spend his thirtieth birthday with friends in New Orleans for Mardi Gras, a popular and expensive time of year to fly there. As soon as Southwest opened up their flight schedule for February, Miguel booked a $375 roundtrip flight from Newark to New Orleans. (Unlike other airlines that start selling flights eleven or twelve months out, Southwest typically does so seven or eight months out.) Even though it wasn't a great price, Miguel knew that he now had eight months to monitor fares. If prices went higher than $375, it didn't matter because he'd already locked in his ticket. If fares went below $375, on either Southwest or another airline, he could cancel the original ticket, book the cheaper flight, and pocket the savings. That's exactly what happened two months later, when a Southwest fare sale dropped the price to $225, saving Miguel $150, which he spent over Mardi Gras in what were undoubtedly clean, wholesome ways.

With *most* airlines you don't want to book flights too early because by doing so you're forgoing potential future price drops. But that principle is premised on the fact that most airlines don't allow changes on their cheapest fares. Because Southwest allows penalty-free changes on their cheapest tickets, locking in a price early ensures that it's *the maximum* you'll pay for flights, and you still have a great chance to get a better deal if the price drops later. It's airfare arbitrage: Heads you win, tails the airline loses.

Southwest is also great for booking trips you're not sure you'll ultimately take. Take my friend Rajan, who is obsessed with Florida Gators football. Though it's been years since they've been legitimate national title contenders, every summer he convinces himself that Next Season Is the One. To that end, as a preseason tradition, he always books himself a January flight to wherever the national championship will be held that year. In 2018, for instance, he paid $300 roundtrip for a flight from Baltimore to San Jose, just in case the Gators made it. If he'd waited until the championship matchup was determined—nine days before the game—fares would likely have been closer to $1,000. Unfortunately for Rajan, Florida lost two games in the first two months, knocking them out of the title race. He canceled his Southwest ticket and got a full refund.

Finally, the free luggage is especially valuable when you're bringing multiple items. A couple of years ago, my wife and I were moving from Colorado to Oregon and had more stuff than we could fit in our car. Instead of paying thousands of dollars for a moving van, we booked a Southwest flight from Denver to

Portland for $150 roundtrip each. Because each ticket included two checked bags and two carry-ons, we were able to schlep eight bags to Portland for $300 total, far less than a moving truck or what it would've cost to ship them. Had we tried to pull the same stunt on United Airlines, we would've paid an additional $30 each for the first checked bag, $40 for the second checked bag, and, because a full-size carry-on isn't permitted with a basic economy ticket, we would've had to check that bag for an absurd $175. Total cost if we'd flown United: $490 for our bags, plus airfare. Assuming similar fares, we saved nearly $500 by using Southwest as our mover instead of United.

Though many people associate Southwest with just domestic flights, they began flying internationally after acquiring AirTran Airways in 2011. At time of writing, Southwest has expanded their route map to include Mexico, Belize, Cuba, Jamaica, the Cayman Islands, Bahamas, Turks and Caicos, Dominican Republic, Puerto Rico, and, most recently, Hawaii. Because all the money-saving perks, from free bags to free flight changes, apply on every Southwest flight, it's always worth searching separately whether you're flying to Milwaukee, Maui, or Montego Bay.

KEY TAKEAWAYS

- Flight search engines, rather than airline websites or OTAs, are the best place to search for cheap flights. It's best to book directly with the airline if prices are the same as an OTA because your ticket gets issued quicker (minimizing the risk your cheap fare disappears), you're protected by the 24-hour rule, and it's simpler to make any changes.

- Although large cities get the highest number of deals, small cities arguably get the highest quality deals. Flights to Europe normally cost much more from Omaha than New York, so a $400 fare from Omaha is much more valuable.

- The line between budget airlines and full-service airlines has increasingly blurred over the years, especially with the introduction of basic economy. Nowadays, add-on fees are common across all airlines (aside from Southwest), regardless of whether they're labeled budget or full service.

- I try to avoid budget airlines not because of fees or onboard experience, but because of the risk of a days-long wait if my flight is canceled. Full-service airlines have partners and far more planes flying, so even a cancellation is unlikely to significantly delay you from reaching your destination.

- Always be aware of add-on fees, read the fine print, and make a plan for avoiding them. Even the same airline can have different fees and restrictions depending on the route.

- Unlike most airlines, Southwest has virtually no add-on fees. Because of free cancellations in particular, it can be useful to make speculative bookings on Southwest. Their fares are found only on their website, though, not on flight search engines or OTAs.

9

CLEAR YOUR COOKIES:
NINE FLIGHT-BOOKING MYTHS DEBUNKED

AIRFARE IS ONE OF THE MOST CONFUSING PURCHASES WE regularly make. Flight prices are both unpredictable (it's impossible to say precisely when a cheap flight to Barcelona will pop up) and seemingly irrational (it's often cheaper to fly from New York to Barcelona than New York to Dayton). Any time something is hard to understand, it inevitably fuels rumors, myths, and misinformation.

"I heard the airlines track your cookies and increase the fare if they know you want to book." "I heard wearing a suit will get me upgraded to first class." "Wait to book your flights until August 23 because that's when they're cheapest."

I wish everyone repeating these wildly incorrect rumors had one head, and I could smack it.

Instead, ever the pacifist, I will do my best to calmly explain why these gossipers and rumormongers are doing you a disservice.

Myth: Clear Your Cookies

Chances are you've heard this suggestion: "Clear your cookies when you're searching for flights because if you search multiple times, the airline will know you really want it and they'll raise the price." It gets repeated again and again. "This is the one thing you should do when searching for flights online," *Business Insider* insisted. *Time* magazine passed along that there's "evidence that this pricing based on search history may not be entirely a myth." *SmarterTravel*'s Ed Hewitt called the evidence "pretty compelling," despite the fact he had "not been able to duplicate this myself." People feel like this has to be true—most websites track your cookies, including airlines, so of course they'd use this information to fiddle with the fares you see, right?

In fact, there are so many reasons it's wrong. First, I've spent hours every day for the better part of the last decade searching for flights and I've never seen any evidence that clearing cookies results in lower fares. Second, it doesn't even make intuitive sense. Most online companies handle abandoned carts— someone who looked at an item but didn't ultimately purchase it—by offering a *discount* rather than raising prices.

The other day I decided to run a little test. I searched for a flight at random, roundtrip from Denver to London between October 6 and October 13. The cheapest fare was $441. I then hit REFRESH and searched again: $441 once more. I spent the next hour doing this again and again and again, 100 times in all. On that 100th search? The fare was still $441. I've run the same experiment on flight search engines, OTAs, and airline websites, all with the same results.

What's important to remember is that airfare can change

by the hour if not by the minute these days. If Super Bowl ticket prices go up while you're pondering whether to go, the simplest explanation is not that the NFL is gouging people like you who are searching. Instead, it's that prices go up because they frequently change. So too with airfare. The fact that a fare sometimes jumps around while you're searching happens not because of your cookies; it happens because airfare is volatile.

The upside here is that there's no downside to clearing your cookies. Just as it won't make flights cheaper, it won't make them more expensive either. Even though airlines aren't tracking cookies to raise prices today, they certainly could start doing so in the future. If you feel better taking the time to clear your cookies or search in an incognito window, you have my permission.

Myth: *The Cheapest Fares Are on Tuesdays at 1 p.m.*

To this day, many websites and news outlets want you to believe there is a single, predictable time of the week when airfare is cheapest to book. FareCompare claims it's Tuesday at 3 p.m. Skyscanner says it's Sunday at 5 a.m. Hopper argues anytime on a Thursday. Expedia swears it's anytime on a Sunday.

The thing about this myth is that it used to be true. Decades ago, when airfare was first available for purchase online, airlines would often load fares onto their system once a week at a specified time, say, Tuesday at 1 p.m. There were only a limited number of the cheapest fares available, so if you were among the first to search after they were loaded, you really could get a good deal.

The problem is that model hasn't been true for years. Nowadays airfare isn't changed once a week; like we explored in Chapter 7, it changes by the day if not by the hour or minute in some cases. And while there are cheaper days of the week to *travel* (Tuesday, Wednesday, and Saturday), there's no cheapest time or day to *book* fares. You may as well try to predict what time next week's biggest news story will break. The fact that four travel companies claim to have studied the matter and arrived at four wildly different conclusions is a glaring tell about whether there's any consistently cheapest time to book.

The bad news is that there's no one time of the week that's cheapest to book. The good news is that cheap flights can—and do—pop up anytime.

Myth: The Cheapest Fares Are on August 23

Similar to the claim that there's a single best time of the week to book cheap flights, some have argued that there's a predictable best day of the year to book cheap flights as well. CheapOair has led this push, declaring August 23 to be "National Cheap Flights Day."

The best way of understanding why this is bogus is to think of the stock market. In 2017, the single best day for stocks was March 1. If your financial adviser told you to put a bunch of money into the market every year on March 1 because that's when the data says stocks will surge, you would've been surprised and upset by the 415-point loss in 2018.

It's the same with cheap flights. You can look back at fares from any given year and pinpoint a single day when they were cheapest, but it doesn't mean that has any predictive power for the following year. Indeed, if someone in 2018 had waited until August 23 to book flights, they would have missed the single best deal all year—$560 roundtrip business class seats to Southeast Asia that normally cost $5,000—that was available on the morning of August 16. Cheap flights pop up all the time; they're not confined to a predictable day.

Myth: Flights Are Only Cheap Because of Coronavirus

When the COVID-19 pandemic first hit the U.S. in early 2020, travelers were agog at some of the fares popping up. Fort Lauderdale to Los Angeles for $26 roundtrip. New York City to Barcelona for $168 roundtrip. Almost no one was looking to travel, but nonetheless, fares like these spread on social media and planted the idea that cheap flights were a result of the pandemic. "The only reason cheap flights are popping up is because no one wants to fly during a pandemic," the thinking went. This logic is understandable, but ultimately incorrect.

As you'll remember from Chapter 6, we've been living in the Golden Age of Cheap Flights for years. The idea that cheap flights only began during the COVID-19 outbreak is pure malarkey. Many of the factors driving down airfare—from improved price discrimination to frequent flyer programs becoming money-printing machines to jet fuel becoming cheaper and cheaper—long predated the pandemic and will continue afterwards.

There's no doubt that COVID-19 initially caused airfare to drop—for example, the $168 fare from New York City to Barcelona was a record low. But it was only $30 less than the $198 roundtrip fare we found in November 2019. And only $9 cheaper than the $177 fare we found from Boston to Barcelona in December 2019.

Myth: The Cheapest Fares Are Last Minute

Thankfully this myth has been mostly buried, but just to be sure, it is absolutely not the case that last-minute deals are plentiful. In fact, airlines tend to jack up prices at the last minute, not cut them.

Like the myth that fares are cheapest on Tuesdays at 1 p.m., this one has the benefit of previously being true. Decades ago, many airlines would cut fares as the departure date approached, reasoning that any empty seat at takeoff was lost potential revenue. Even $50 was better than $0, right?

Beginning with a 1972 academic paper from a researcher with British Airways, airlines began waking up to the fact that passengers booking last-minute tickets were predominantly businesspeople who didn't schedule meetings months in advance the way leisure travelers schedule vacations. And because it was their company paying, not them, business travelers didn't care how expensive fares were. As a result, airlines realized they'd make more money if they *raised* prices in the last few weeks before departure, even if that meant flying with some empty seats.

Myth: Dressing Nicely Will Get You an Upgrade

One of the main reasons airlines have gotten so profitable in recent years—and have been able to afford flying economy passengers to Europe for under $300 roundtrip—is that they've gotten much better at selling business and first class seats. In 2011, Delta sold 13 percent of its first class seats; by 2019, it sold 60 percent.

When there are unsold premium seats, airlines have gotten much more formulaic about designating who will get them. Many airlines solicit cash upgrade bids during check-in, and any leftover empty seats are awarded complimentary to passengers with top-tier elite status. If there are more empty seats than elite travelers, airlines are happy to leave the seats unfilled, lest they give passengers the impression they can get a business class seat for free by holding out long enough.

Which is all to say the old lore of sweet-talking and sweet-dressing your way into a first class seat isn't going to work nowadays.

Myth: Wait for Advertised Sales

When an airline advertises a sale, especially on international flights, it's almost never worth your time.

Think about how marketing works at its core: A company is trying to convince you to buy something. When an airline has $950 fares to Paris, it has to convince people it's a good deal. But $250 fares to Paris need no marketing dollars. A fare that good sells itself. Plus, when an airline quietly runs a sale, it has a lot more flexibility about how long and how far it drops fares because it doesn't have an entire advertising campaign running.

You can safely ignore when an airline's marketing department tries to convince you its latest fares are hot hot hot. Instead, it's the *unadvertised* sales that are the real gold mines.

Myth: One Airline Is Always Cheapest

I often get asked some variation of "What airline is cheapest for flights to London?" or "What's the cheapest route to get to Vietnam?" The answer: There isn't one. The cheapest fare on any given route is shuffling around every day; there's no consistent, predictably cheapest airline on a given route. Rather than trying to anticipate which airline has the best fare, use a flight search engine or OTA (see Chapter 8) to compare across all airlines.

Myth: Flying Was Way Better Back in the Day

Though not a flight-booking myth per se, this is a bee in my travel bonnet nonetheless. Mid-twentieth-century air travel—widely revered as the golden age of flying—was actually terrible.

Flying was incredibly expensive; in 1948, a TWA flight from New York City to Rome cost $848 roundtrip, or more than $9,000 today. (The same flight today can go as low as $248 roundtrip.) Flights also took far longer; New York to Rome used to be a 20-hour trip; nowadays it's 8 hours. Even the poshest seats weren't all that comfortable; they were more akin to modern premium economy seats than the lie-flat seats invented in the late 1990s. Forget about WiFi or personal seatback TV screens with the latest movies and shows. Though food and drinks were abundant and complimentary, diners also had to deal with cigarette smoke wafting throughout the cabin. Planes crashed constantly. And when they weren't falling out of the sky, they were being perpetually hijacked, sometimes multiple times a day. Minorities were not allowed to fly until the 1960s. Women who applied to work as flight attendants faced preposterous levels of sexism and misogyny, including restrictions on age (21 to 26), height (5'2" to 5'6"), weight (100 to 130 pounds), and marital status (single).

The idea that flying was better back in the day is an unambiguous example of revisionist history. It's akin to romanticizing the good old days of wagon travel, or how great it must have been sailing with Magellan. The experience would be unthinkable for humans of modern tastes.

KEY TAKEAWAYS

- Because airfare is unlike anything else we purchase, there is a lot of outdated or downright false advice on how to get good deals.
- The idea that clearing your cookies will lead to lower fares is one of the most widely believed myths, but there's no evidence to support it. The good news is that clearing your cookies won't make flights more expensive.
- Many idiosyncrasies that were once true—like there being a predictably cheapest time to book flights or last-minute fares getting slashed—are no longer accurate.

10

SHOULD YOU TAKE THAT TRIP? HOW TO THINK ABOUT OVERTOURISM AND EMISSIONS

WHILE EXPLORING THE WORLD IS GRAND AND IMPORTANT, travelers have become increasingly cognizant of some of its negative effects. Pollution. Tourists behaving poorly. Wholesale changes to local neighborhoods. As the number of travelers has exploded, so too has society's awareness of the issues that mass tourism can cause.

I want to focus our discussion here on two central concerns in the modern travel debate: airplane emissions and overtourism. While I have a stronger personal opinion on the matter of overtourism, my goal in this chapter isn't to give you any definitive answers but, rather, to give you more context so you can make informed decisions for yourself.

To begin with, while we all love to travel, many of us are left to wonder: Is my vacation hurting the planet? Climate change is a massive threat that's only growing worse, and airplanes are a notable source of greenhouse gases. As of 2019, airplanes were responsible for 2.4 percent of global carbon dioxide emissions, as well as other harmful outputs like nitrogen oxides and soot. (By comparison, industrial heat accounts for 10 percent of the world's emissions, but when was the last time you heard criticism of that?) While airplane emissions are small in a relative sense, there are two major reasons to be concerned.

First, emissions from planes are particularly difficult to eliminate. While renewably sourced electricity is increasingly powering our cars and homes, passenger planes will continue to rely on jet fuel for the foreseeable future. For a variety of reasons, large electric jets just aren't realistic anytime soon. And while taking the train is a much greener form of transportation, most of the world isn't connected by high-speed rail infrastructure (including, rather crucially, the ocean).

Second, the number of flights is growing rapidly. As the middle class expands not just in China and India but throughout the world, so too does the demand for air travel. According to the International Air Transport Association, by 2037 the number of passengers worldwide is projected to double.

Air travel and the environment isn't all bad news; there are some mitigating factors as well. For starters, new aircraft are more fuel-efficient than previous generations. Modern airport logistics are reducing the amount of fuel wasted by planes idling before takeoff. Some airlines like United are adding greener biofuels to the mix, while others like Delta and JetBlue are pledging to become carbon neutral. And most significant, the United Nations has created a framework (known as the Carbon Offsetting and Reduction Scheme for International Aviation, or CORSIA) to hold aviation emissions at recent levels through a mix of efficiency gains and carbon offsets.

In the meantime, as airlines send more planes into the sky and take steps to limit their impact, how should you as a traveler feel about your next flight? Fortunately, there's a bit of good news: The cheaper your flight, the less harmful it is for the environment.

CHEAPER FLIGHTS = FEWER FLIGHTS = LESS CULPABILITY

One of the biggest misconceptions is that every passenger on a flight contributes equally to that plane's emissions. It's simply not true, nor is it true that all passengers in the same *cabin* are equally culpable. To illustrate why, let's walk through a mental experiment.

Imagine Southwest is about to fly a 150-seat plane to Boston with 149 passengers on board and they offer you a free ticket for the final empty seat. From a purely environmental standpoint, how should you feel about taking it?

There are two primary factors to consider: Will your physically being there cause the plane to burn more fuel? And will your presence incentivize the airline to add more flights?

An airplane's emissions come from burning jet fuel, and the heavier the plane, the more fuel it needs to fly. That said, because airplanes are already so massive, the amount of extra fuel needed for an additional person on board is virtually none. *FiveThirty-Eight* estimated that a 160-pound person flying between Denver and Boston would add a marginal fuel cost of about $8, or a few gallons of jet fuel. When I lived in Fort Collins, I needed that amount of gas just to make the hour-long drive to the Denver airport. So if that Southwest plane was going to fly whether or not you're on board, accepting a free ticket won't make the flight more harmful.

Even if your presence won't cause a real increase in a plane's greenhouse gases, there's still the question of whether you're indirectly adding emissions by giving an airline incentive to add more flights. Getting a good answer here requires thinking about your ticket from the airline's perspective.

Imagine a Southwest executive is looking at revenue from your Boston flight and trying to decide whether to add an extra plane each day. The fact that the airline couldn't sell the 150th seat is a red flag. After all, why would Southwest want to add capacity on a route they're already having trouble selling out?

Now imagine that executive is looking at a different flight to Dallas, where instead of giving away the 150th seat, they were able to sell it for $900. That's a highly profitable customer. If the executive sees that the final passenger to Dallas generated $900, and the final passenger to Boston generated $0, where is she going to add an extra flight?

Obviously, this is a highly simplified example, but it's instructive nonetheless: The less you paid for your ticket, the less incentive you give the airline to fly more. While a free ticket is fanciful, the same takeaway holds when you pay $300 to visit Copenhagen. On the contrary, if you buy a $2,000 last-minute fare, that encourages the airline to add another Copenhagen flight because they feel more confident that the additional flight will be profitable.

Of course, airlines aren't making decisions about capacity based on the behavior of a single individual (a fact that may alleviate personal guilt about taking a flight in the first place). You may be worried your presence is incentivizing the airline to fly more, but your impact largely depends on how much you paid. Because cheaper flights mean fewer flights mean less carbon, you can feel less bad about an airplane's environmental impact when you got a good deal on the ticket.

Further, it's not just how much you paid that impacts your responsibility for a flight's emissions but also where you sit. Even setting aside the relationship between airfare and emissions, it's still the case that some passengers are more culpable than others. To understand why, let's compare your Southwest flight with Billionaire Bill's private flight.

Though the exact amount of emissions depends on various factors including weather and routing, let's assume your Southwest 737 plane emits around 40 metric tons of carbon dioxide. In the most simplistic view, if there are 150 passengers on board, that means the plane gave off 0.27 metric tons of emissions per passenger. Billionaire Bill, meanwhile, took his mistress on a private jet to Boston. With just two passengers, the plane's emissions work out to 20 metric tons per person. By flying private, Bill and Darlene were responsible for 74 times more emissions per passenger than passengers on the Southwest flight.

Now let's do that same exercise but for folks sitting in different cabins of the same plane, in this case a Singapore Airlines A380. The plane's 343 economy seats each take up about 4 square feet, while the 44 premium economy seats occupy about 5 square feet apiece. The fully reclining business seats, meanwhile, come in around 11.5 square feet each, and the first class suites—which are large enough for a bed *alongside* the seat—size up at 20 square feet.

The fact that 5 economy travelers could fit in the space af-

forded 1 first class passenger isn't just a story about societal inequality; it's also about environmental inequality. An A380 is
a large enough plane to fit 868 economy seats, but because premium seats take up extra space, a Singapore Airlines A380 carries
a maximum of 475 passengers. If 800 passengers wanted to fly
to London, an all-economy A380 would only have to make one
journey, while a plane with premium cabins would have to make
the trek twice—roughly double the emissions. Premium seating
is certainly more comfortable, but it's less efficient and less green.

Don't just take it from me; when the World Bank conducted
a study on the matter, it found that first class passengers had a
carbon footprint up to 9 times larger than travelers sitting in
coach. Given these findings, it's no surprise that in 2019 when
researchers from the International Council on Clean Transportation studied which U.S. airlines were the greenest—moving
the most passengers per gallon of jet fuel—the winners were
Frontier, Spirit, and Southwest: all budget airlines without spa-
cious first class seats.

Zooming out from which types of fares bear the most culpability for a plane's emissions, there's a larger question: Should
we even be placing the burden of solving climate change on the
back of your vacation?

FLIGHT EMISSIONS: AN INDIVIDUAL OR COLLECTIVE RESPONSIBILITY? (OR BOTH?)

A central question in tackling climate change is whether we
should focus on changing individuals' behavior, or should we
seek to change society-wide behavior?

At its crux, this question boils down to two factors: chance of success and amount of impact. How likely is it that a desired outcome will come to fruition, and, if it does, how much will it matter? For instance, when you decide to bike somewhere instead of drive, the outcome is certain (you successfully saved gas), while the impact is low (the amount of emissions saved is minuscule on a global scale).

Let's think about success and impact in the context of your flight. Although choosing to fly less will have a negligible impact on the environment, there's a guarantee of success. Climate change is such an overwhelming problem, and it feels productive to accomplish something, especially considering that for most people, a flight is the single largest contributor to their personal carbon footprints. And because most trips, especially vacations, are discretionary, there can be a sense that the moral thing to do is fly less—or stop flying altogether.

At the same time, looking narrowly at the carbon footprint of your flight can leave out some important context. Let me use a personal example. I certainly take more flights than the average American, but I also rarely drive, I pay extra for renewable electricity, I never buy new clothes (my mother-in-law sews sock holes, bless her), I write weekly meal plans to prevent food waste, and I support higher taxes to fight climate change. Am I worse for the planet than someone who drives a ton and buys a lot of stuff but doesn't fly overseas?

It's not that individual choices don't have an impact on the climate but, rather, that your choices alone aren't enough. You, the reader, could live the perfect green life, never release a single extra gram of carbon than was necessary, and it wouldn't do any more to reverse climate change than a squirt gun will put out a forest fire. At the same time, if *everyone* lived sustainably, it would of course make a huge difference. As Maria Bustillos at *Popula* argues, "Collective action doesn't fall off a tree, it is made up of countless individual acts." The tricky part is convincing billions of people to follow your lead.

The argument against thinking of climate change as a personal responsibility isn't about ignoring the science. It's true that the planet is getting warmer and it's true that planes add carbon into the atmosphere. What's up for debate is whether individual action is up to the task at hand. As *New York Magazine*'s Eric Levitz notes, "If you accept the scientific consensus on warming, then you know your personal carbon footprint is a drop in the rising sea. So, why on earth would you feel compelled to lower your quality of life for the sake of cutting carbon emissions by a wholly negligible amount?" Under this line of thinking, any amount of effort spent greening your own life would perhaps be better spent calling political leaders and demanding better climate policies. The fate of our planet depends on political choices, not your flight to Paris.

Even Representative Alexandria Ocasio-Cortez, architect of the Green New Deal, has pushed back against the idea that you can't get on an airplane if you support a cleaner environment. "Living in the world as it is isn't an argument against working towards a better future," she tweeted in 2019.

Why not both personal and *collective responsibility?* you may be wondering. In fact, a Stanford researcher named Seth Werfel looked at this very question. Following the 2011 Fukushima nuclear disaster, Japanese citizens were encouraged to curb their personal energy use. Afterward, Werfel surveyed 12,000 people to ask about their support for a carbon tax and made a surprising discovery: The more an individual personally limited their consumption, the less likely they were to support a carbon tax. "At first, I thought this result was counterintuitive," Werfel explained. "But it is intuitive, just not obvious. When . . . people feel like they'd done enough, they said that the government shouldn't make them do more."

To be clear, individual action to fight climate change is laudable. Is it impactful enough to bend the arc of global warming? That's an exceedingly difficult challenge, because asking people to stop flying is asking them to stop traveling in a modern, recognizable way. What keeps so many of us going through the day-in day-out drudgery at work is that next vacation. And though we may not love flights or their emissions, until scientists finally get around to inventing teleportation, it's the only realistic way to travel overseas.

Even if flight emissions are hard to stymie and stopping travel is a nonstarter, is there promise in counteracting air travel with carbon offsets?

CARBON OFFSETS

Because airline emissions are so difficult to eliminate, yet we need flights for most overseas travel, one widely adopted approach is to reduce greenhouse gases *elsewhere* to compensate for your trip. This is known as carbon offsetting— counterbalancing your share of a flight's emissions by putting money toward a carbon-reducing project like planting trees, building solar farms, replacing inefficient cooking stoves, or preserving forests.

In theory, carbon offsets are an eloquent and effective solution. If a plane emits a pound of carbon dioxide and a preserved acre of forest sucks up a pound of carbon dioxide, from an environmental standpoint it's a wash. In practice, though, offsets have had an inconsistent record.

For offsets to work, they must satisfy three requirements: additionality, permanence, and leakage. First, was that new windmill built *because of* offset money, and would it not have happened otherwise? Second, will those new trees, which were planted thanks to offset money, not be cut down in a few years (thus releasing all their stored carbon into the atmosphere)? And finally, will the section of forest you paid to preserve just push loggers to cut down the next patch over?

Faulty carbon offset schemes, of which there are many, fail one or more of these questions. As a 2019 ProPublica investigation titled "Why Carbon Credits for Forest Preservation May Be Worse Than Nothing" uncovered:

> In case after case, I found that carbon credits hadn't offset the amount of pollution they were supposed to, or they had brought gains that were quickly reversed or that couldn't be accurately measured to begin with. Ultimately, the polluters got a guilt-free pass to keep emitting CO_2, but the forest preservation that was supposed to balance the ledger either never came or didn't last.

Given these widespread issues, critics argue that offsets are more akin to medieval Catholic indulgences: less about solving the problem than absolving our guilt.

To be sure, there are good offsets and bad offsets, and in general new projects are superior to ones that were first launched years ago. We have better satellite technology to monitor forest preservation today than we did a decade ago and improved independent third-party verification. But even with the best tools, administering offsets effectively remains tricky.

Another issue at play is how to properly price carbon. Most carbon footprint calculators are simplistic, just taking into account how long your flight is and using that to determine how much carbon you should offset. But this is problematic for two reasons. First, it's imprecise to say each person on a flight—or even in the same cabin—is equally culpable for the flight's emissions. Like we discussed, a flight with one empty seat burns virtually the same fuel as a completely full flight; you, a cheap flight aficionado who paid a pittance, aren't as responsible for the flight's emissions as your seatmate who paid full price. Second, if we've accurately calculated how much carbon each passenger is responsible for, it's still highly contentious what the price of carbon ought to be. There's no single agreed-upon answer, and estimates range from $10 per ton to $100 or more.

Even if we're able to create an effective offset project and decide on an appropriate standard price, there's still the issue of usage to consider. Right now, offsetting your flight is entirely voluntary. As such, there's a tragedy of the commons dynamic at play. We'd all be better off working together to combat climate change, but it's in no individual's personal interest to buy carbon offsets if others are taking a pass. It's no wonder only one in ten Americans has *ever* purchased an offset. (The dynamic is a bit different for airlines, which get a PR benefit from purchasing carbon offsets, as many have begun doing.)

In the end, most scientists and environmentalists will concede that while offsets aren't flawless, climate change is such an immense problem that any action to combat it is better than no action. Emissions aren't the only negative externality that travelers are asked to consider these days, though; there's also the issue of whether our presence is ruining some destinations.

IS OVERTOURISM BAD?

Over the past few years, as cheap flights have become more prolific and more people have been able to see the world, a backlash has emerged. "Too Many People Want to Travel" proclaimed *The Atlantic*. "The accessible price of travel in Europe has become a problem for locals and visitors alike," argued *Bloomberg*. Virtually nonexistent before 2018, articles decrying "overtourism" are everywhere now.

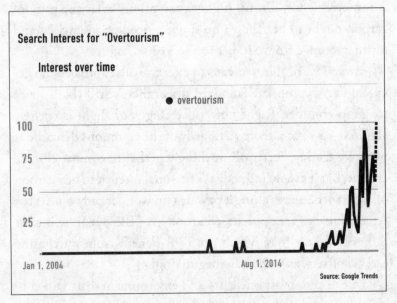

Search Interest for "Overtourism"

Interest over time

● overtourism

Jan 1, 2004   Aug 1, 2014

Source: Google Trends

The criticism generally centers on one of two factors: tourists behaving badly and neighborhoods changing as visitors rush in. Travelers who deface sacred spots certainly deserve scorn, but all it takes is a quick scan of any town's police Twitter feed or Florida Man headlines to disabuse yourself of the notion that poor conduct is confined to visitors. The question of changing neighborhoods is far more nuanced and complex than we have room for here—touching on everything from zoning policy to taxes to a philosophical question of whether development is Actually Good or Actually Bad—but one undeniable factor is that neighborhoods are always changing and always have been. They're less a monument, carved in stone, and more a slowly changing river, constantly redrawing itself to meet the moment.

What bothers me about much of the overtourism discussion is that it's premised on the notion that tourism was only sustainable when it was a playground for the wealthy. Too many people are now able to visit the world's most iconic destinations—and that's a problem, the thinking goes.

I couldn't disagree more. For most of the two centuries that modern tourism has existed, it's been walled off from the masses. Princes and plutocrats have long been able to admire the Leaning Tower of Pisa and explore the Pyramids of Giza; everyone else was resigned to reading about them in textbooks. How lucky are we, today, to be living in the Golden Age of Cheap Flights, when international travel is no longer reserved for nobility? To me, that's worth celebrating, not decrying. Travel is a wondrous thing, and it's wonderful that it's being democratized.

Sure, some popular spots can get crowded, but one fun part of spending ten hours on a flight is witnessing with your own eyes how massive the world is. Even today, at the apex of overtourism concerns, most of the world remains uncrowded. If you find dealing with the masses loathsome, don't go to Disney World or the Louvre. I've never been to either, and I wouldn't say my travel career has been deprived. There are plenty of other amusement parks and museums.

It can be disappointing, of course, when a favorite place gets discovered by reams of others, but that's a part of living in society. Tourists don't own their favorite sites; it's not for them to keep others out. Getting upset because of long lines at the Eiffel Tower makes about as much sense as one snowflake blaming all the others for causing an avalanche.

I'm not arguing that every world-class site should tear down its gates and let millions of people in at once. There's clearly a need for regulation and protection so future generations can continue to enjoy these places. Many local governments are having success with measures like tourism taxes, congestion pricing, and other efforts to promote sustainable travel. I'm all in support.

But one bad solution is shaming people for wanting to travel, especially considering all its benefits for both tourists and hosts. Some would have you believe that either tourists win, or locals win, but never both. On the contrary, tourism isn't a zero-sum game; it can help protect and bolster localities. By one estimate, over 10 percent of jobs in the world are supported by tourism, including popular U.S. destinations like Hawaii, Las Vegas, and Orlando. Those tourist dollars not only provide a living for millions but also help ensure that natural lands across the globe, from national parks to the Serengeti, don't get razed or plundered. As sustainable tourism expert Costas Christ wrote in the *New York Times* about what might happen without tourism: "Save the elephants? Forget about it."

I witnessed this firsthand during my $130 Milan trip when I took a train out to Cinque Terre, the illustrious string of Italian seaside villages. After arriving in one of the hamlets, Manarola, I stopped in at a small bed-and-breakfast for a snack. I got to chatting with the waitress whose family, it turned out, owned the place. What was it like working in a place so popular with tourists? I asked. It was wonderful, she said, to my surprise. Growing up, when few tourists made it to Cinque Terre, she dreaded that a lack of local economic opportunity meant she would eventually have to move to Milan in search of work. Instead, the tourism boom felt like a miracle because it allowed her to stay in Manarola and raise a family there.

Though visitors behaving poorly and damaging local treasures grabs our attention, in reality, *not enough tourism* is a far larger threat. When tourism money is on the line, that financial incentive makes it easier to maintain the sanctity of a destination. If a site loses that influx of visitors, it's significantly more likely to fall into a state of disrepair, but it will do so gradually over time, without the rage-inducing headlines generated by ill-behaved tourists.

Far from being a guilty pleasure, travel is best thought of as a civic responsibility. You can learn about your family's lineage from a DNA test, but that report won't compare to the feeling of visiting your motherland, walking the grounds your ancestors did. You can read about the Khmer Rouge, but it won't compare to the horror of walking around the Killing Fields, seeing shards of clothing still emerge after every rain, forty years later. Watching Anthony Bourdain wax poetic about bun cha isn't the same as tasting the truly life-changing northern Vietnamese dish for yourself.

Travel can feel like an indulgent activity, but I prefer the philosophy of Rick Steves that it's actually something you owe to others: learning about other cultures, seeing others' lives and homelands, experiencing what's important to them. Gone are the days when we all grew up, got married, worked, and died, never interacting with the broader world. From climate change to culture to globalization to food, we're far more connected than we used to be. Understanding one another, and sharing the humanity that knows no borders, is both a simple courtesy and a mounting necessity.

KEY TAKEAWAYS

- Air travel accounts for 2.4 percent of global carbon emissions. Underlying that number is the fact that airplane emissions are particularly difficult to eliminate, and they're growing quickly, though efforts are underway to limit net carbon output.

- Culpability for a plane's emissions varies widely among passengers. Responsibility doesn't vary just by cabin but also by ticket price. Travelers who got a cheap fare are disproportionately less blameworthy for emissions because they gave the airline little financial incentive to add an additional flight.

- There's an ongoing debate about whether climate change is best tackled at the individual or societal level. Though both are likely necessary and then some, even the Green New Deal architect agrees that it's not hypocritical to get on an airplane if you care about fighting climate change.

- Carbon offsets are one way to tackle the difficulty of eliminating airplane emissions. They work in theory, but in practice they can be tricky to pull off effectively, especially when they're a voluntary individual solution.

- As international travel has become more mainstream, so too have worries about overtourism. While logistical concerns are warranted, much of the criticism is overblown. Travel is not an inherently zero-sum activity but, rather, a mutually beneficial endeavor that we should celebrate, especially as it becomes available to more and more people.

11

THE UNEXPECTED JOYS OF TRAVEL: HOW TO GET BETTER AT VACATIONING

THE MORE YOU PAINT, THE BETTER YOUR ARTWORK. THE more you cook, the better your meals. The more you run, the better your endurance.

Travel is no different.

We think of vacationing solely as an escape from the monotony of daily life: a break from our jobs, our lives, something different. But travel is more than that. It's a skill set. The better we become at it, the more joy we get from exploring the world. It's not an innate talent. We're not born knowing how to navigate airports or foreign neighborhoods. We don't immediately grasp on our very first trip what aspects of travel make us happiest.

Instead, vacationing is an activity at which you get better with experience. There are a few reasons why.

First, the more flights you take, the better you understand the minutiae of air travel. Booking flights is intimidating, even for seasoned travelers. Can we really expect people booking their first flight to understand that their fare probably doesn't include a checked bag or that they have to pay huge fees if they cancel their ticket? Each booking we make leaves us more informed, better prepared, and less stressed for the next one—like muscle memory, but for flights.

Second, the more you fly, the better you get at using tips and tricks to get good fares. I shudder remembering the exorbitant prices I paid early in my travel life. More than $1,000 roundtrip to get down to Chile—what was I thinking? Today, I'd wait patiently for a better fare, or fly somewhere significantly cheaper nearby, or use any of the dozens of other strategies detailed in this book. Back then, I didn't know any better.

Third, the more you travel, the better you get at navigating foreign places. Your first trip overseas can be intimidating. Your tenth trip? Less so. Each time, you get a bit more confident at stumbling through foreign languages, figuring out local customs, and finding your way to Point B. You know you'll be fine on the next trip because you made it through this one.

Fourth, and perhaps most fascinating: The more we venture out, the better we get at discerning what we hate and what we love about traveling so we can structure future trips accordingly. Think of someone reading novels for the first time. If it's a mystery book and she hates it, it's not that she necessarily hates reading; she may just dislike mystery as a genre. Mysteries aren't for everyone, nor is romance or sci-fi. It can be hard to predict who will like what; you've got to open a few books to see what's inside.

Early in my travel life, I used to pack my schedule so tight with tours and activities that I would come home more wound up than when I left. The first time we traveled together, my then-girlfriend, now-wife nudged me to reconsider. "Do you think we could try going with the flow a bit more?" she asked one evening. I'd never really considered doing less on vacation, because I was terrified of missing something. But she was absolutely right. By relaxing and allowing for some serendipity in our schedule, I found myself enjoying travel far more.

Turns out many travelers undergo the same experience. A 1998 study from Waikato University in New Zealand looked at the reasons why vacationers wanted to travel (to relax, adventure, have fun, et cetera) and how their past experiences impacted their enjoyment of a trip. The study found that "the intellectual motivations for holidaying are generally consistent, but that [travelers], through experience, get better at meeting those needs." In other words, frequent travelers are better at formulating trips that they personally will enjoy.

As we travel more, what we look to get out of our trips evolves as well. Tourism professor Philip Pearce coined the concept of a Travel Career Pattern to describe the way our motivations for travel shift as we gain more experience. While travelers of all levels are equally motivated by having fun, relaxing, and strengthening personal relationships, there's a host of other factors that tend to drive experienced and inexperienced travelers differently. For less experienced travelers, the most salient motivators include boosting self-confidence, exploring the unknown, gaining a new perspective on life, and learning more about oneself, as well as showing off one's travels to others. More experienced travelers, meanwhile, are more likely to prize factors like being in nature, learning new things, and experiencing different cultures. (Not *all* travel pros are nature lovers, nor are *all* novices traveling in order to humblebrag—this is just on average.)

In 2009, when I returned home after visiting Europe for the

first time, I was so enthralled by the experience that I made my friend sit down and look through each of the six hundred photos I'd taken. (Thanks—and sorry, Sarah.) Coming from a small town in Ohio, it was important to me, consciously or subconsciously, that my friends recognize me as the type of person who visits Europe.

Now that I've traveled overseas many times, I rarely post about my trips on social media or anywhere else. Other factors motivate me more nowadays, from spending time with family to trying local foods. Just like what motivated me in my twenties was different from what drove me in my thirties, so too I anticipate that my interests and needs will continue to evolve with each new trip.

Over the years, I've changed the way I travel to let serendipity play a much larger role during vacations. It wasn't an easy transition. My natural state is hyperorganized, doing my best to make an unpredictable world predictable. Improvising is tough for me in any capacity, much less one that feels as important and weighty as travel. If I didn't plan out every hour of my trip, what if I missed something and it was my one chance? My fear—and it's one that I think most travelers and nontravelers share—was that I'd wind up with regrets.

TRAVELING WITHOUT REGRETS

In 1986, future Nobel laureate Daniel Kahneman and Dale T. Miller ran an experiment. They posed the following scenario to a group of subjects:

Mr. Paul owns shares in company A. During the past year he *considered switching to stock in company B, but he decided against it. He now finds out that he would have been better off by $1,200 if he had switched to the stock of company B.*

Mr. George owned shares in company B. During the past year he switched to stock in company A. He now finds that he would have been better off by $1,200 if he had kept his stock in company B.

Who feels greater regret?

Of the 138 respondents, 92 percent said they thought Mr. George would have more regret. Even though the two men found themselves in the exact same position—$1,200 poorer than they could have been—we assume that Mr. George would feel worse because he wound up poorer after being proactive, as opposed to Mr. Paul, who passively missed out.

The fear of misfortune can paralyze us and stop us from taking action. What if we're Mr. George and that stock trade goes south? What if we take that trip to Turkey and it's not as much fun as we'd hoped? Think of the self-recriminations! It's no wonder most people have a well-established preference for the status quo.

This begs the question: Whether in stocks or travel, would we be happier if we didn't take risks?

Eight years after Kahneman and Miller's study, two Cornell professors, Thomas Gilovich and Victoria Husted Medvec, looked deeper into what causes regret and how that's impacted by the passage of time. They ran a new experiment, similar to Kahneman and Miller's, but this time posing the hypothetical of two college students considering transferring schools. Dave ultimately decides to stay, while Jim decides to transfer.

"Suppose their decisions turn out badly for both of them," Gilovich and Medvec posited. "Dave still doesn't like it where he is and wishes he had transferred, and Jim doesn't like his new environment and wishes he had stayed." Respondents were then asked who they thought would experience more regret. As in Kahneman and Miller's study, the overwhelming majority thought the person who took action and wound up unhappy (Jim) would have more to lament. A funny thing happened, though, when respondents were asked who would have the most regrets *in the long run*: It flipped. Whereas 76 percent initially thought it would be Jim, in the long run 64 percent said Dave would have more remorse.

When we take a risk and it turns out poorly, we do have regrets, but those regrets tend to be short-lived. The lasting ones that stick with us over the years, on the other hand, stem from risks we *didn't* take. "Actions produce greater regret in the short term, whereas inactions generate more regret in the long run," Gilovich and Medvec concluded.

This is apparent when the two researchers asked older folks to look back on their lives and think about their biggest laments. Among senior citizens, 74 percent of their regrets stemmed from things they chose *not* to do. We think we're going to wish we hadn't taken a new job or broken off a relationship or traveled somewhere unfamiliar, when in reality it's the opportunities we let slip by that engender lasting remorse.

Think of how regret impacts our travel lives. "Should I go to South Korea, even though I don't speak the language?" "Should I try this foreign dish I've never heard of?" "I don't know much about Ethiopia's customs, would it be intimidating to take a trip there?" Many of us ponder these questions and let ourselves get hamstrung by *anticipated* regret. But it's not mistranslations and bad meals that we bemoan in the long run. Instead, what so many of us wish, especially as we get older, is that we'd traveled more when we had the chance.

Rather than asking yourself if you'll regret taking a trip you're considering, ask yourself this: How many trips have you taken in your life that you wish you hadn't? For most of us, the answer is none, even for trips that didn't go particularly well.

I've had plenty of bad moments traveling. That time I slept on a cement dock in Portugal because I couldn't find anywhere with an available bed. That time I went to catch a train in Germany, only to find out all the public transportation workers were on strike. Bouts with food poisoning in Cambodia, Indonesia, and Mexico.

These experiences were awful in the moment, yet like many distressing ordeals, their salience diminished quickly. With a bit of time, the episodes shifted in my mind from manifestly unpleasant to nostalgic memories. They became a part of my character, a line or two of text in the story of my life that's more interesting to recount than a trip where nothing went awry because no risks were taken—or because I never boarded the plane at all.

It's not that we should try to have an omnishambles trip in the hopes that it will be more memorable. Rather, it's that we shouldn't let fear of bad travel experiences prevent us from getting out there. As my father once wrote, "The calamities of our lives give us interesting memories to mull, far more interesting than the void of ventures not pursued." If you didn't get what you wanted, at least you got a good story.

If I'm prompted to think of the regrets in my travel life, it's not the missed trains and food poisonings that come to mind. I regret the India flights I took too long to book and just missed out on. I wish I'd gone running with the bulls in Spain when a younger me had the opportunity. I should have spent more time exploring Colorado's mountains when I lived there.

In the end, it's the trips we don't take that result in the most regrets. Taking more vacations—and using cheap flights to visit more off-the-beaten-path destinations, as we discussed in Chapter 2—is a sound way to ensure that the regrets you have in fifty years won't include "I wish I had traveled more when I had the chance."

There's an added benefit to planning more trips as well: the anticipation.

THE HAPPIEST PART OF TRAVEL IS ANTICIPATION

I know what you're thinking. The idea that it's more fun looking forward to your vacation than actually being on it feels preposterous. How could daydreaming about snorkeling in the Caribbean or eating gelato in Italy be better than actually snorkeling or eating? And what about all the great memories we make, reflecting back on the colorful fish and tasty sweets?

Yet in study after study, researchers have found that people's happiness about a trip peaks *before* they leave. In 1997, a group of social scientists from Northwestern, George Washington University, Mount Vernon Nazarene College, and the University of Washington conducted an experiment with three sets of vacationers. The first group embarked on a 12-day guided tour of Europe, the second enjoyed a Thanksgiving break from university, and the third took a 3-week bicycle trip around California. In each of the three groups, respondents gave their highest marks about the vacation before the trip, a phenomenon known as rosy prospection. It turns out we look forward to the trip more than we actually enjoy being on the trip.

If that's the case, then would we be happier just not traveling at all? In 2010, Dutch researchers examined this question, comparing the happiness levels of vacationers with nonvacationers. It turns out that prior to a trip, vacationers reported significantly higher happiness scores compared to nonvacationers. For travelers, researchers concluded, "The enjoyment starts weeks, even months before the holiday actually begins."

It's not just the prospect of a trip itself that gives us joy. We associate travel with happiness, so in a tautological, almost Calvinistic manner, just the mere act of booking yourself a trip makes you happy because you become the type of person who travels rather than stays home. There's an element of keeping up with the Joneses: "People who anticipate a holiday feel to be better off than those who intend to stay at home," the Dutch researchers wrote.

To be clear, it's not as though we don't have fun on vacations. Studies show that people do enjoy themselves on trips. Nobody would argue that being on vacation is a chore or a bore. But we tend to overestimate how much fun we'll have during a trip and underappreciate how impactful the lead-up to a vacation can be.

You may be saying to yourself, *Maybe other people enjoy the anticipation more than the actual trip, but not me.* To which I say, Great! There's an unavoidably circuitous link between anticipation and enjoyment. You wouldn't savor the anticipation of something you don't think you'll enjoy. By reminding yourself of how much you relish being on vacation, you're also increasing your anticipation for the next trip.

If the anticipation of travel is more enjoyable than traveling itself, what does that mean for trip planning? To begin with, we should try to solidify travel plans further out. The idea of a last-minute spontaneous trip—especially the proverbial show-up-at-the-airport-and-pick-somewhere idea—has always had a romantic allure. But the less planning time you afford yourself, the less enjoyment you're giving yourself. If anticipation is the happiest part, we should seek to lengthen, not shorten, the pre-trip period.

I'm reminded of Shakespeare's declaration in *Julius Caesar* that "cowards die many times before their deaths," except that for our purposes, a traveler lives her trip many times before stepping onto the plane. When we think we're going to enjoy something, wittingly or not, we are coaxing ourselves into enjoying it more than we would have otherwise. We interpret the trip in a rosier light, we confirm our biases.

This isn't just true of travel. Humans derive pleasure from anticipating all types of experiences. For example, a 1987 study conducted by a University of Chicago researcher asked participants how much they would pay to kiss their favorite celebrity. Turns out people will pay more for that kiss three days from now than they would pay for an immediate kiss. Similarly, a 2014 study from Cornell, UC Berkeley, and UC San Francisco compared how people react to delayed purchases of experiences and material things. "Waiting for an experience elicits significantly more happiness, pleasantness, and excitement than waiting for a material good," the researchers found. "Consumers derive value from anticipation."

Extending your travel planning has additional knock-on effects. A 2018 study conducted by the U.S. Travel Association found that "planners are happier than nonplanners in every category measured," including work, relationships, health, and vacation satisfaction. In addition, planners were more likely to take their full vacation allotment than nonplanners. One major reason why: You're *much* more likely to get the time off if you request it six months in advance than if you ask for vacation time next week. (There are more than forty employees at Scott's Cheap Flights, each of whom loves to travel, and I can tell you unequivocally that early vacation requests are the easiest to approve.)

But Scott, you may be wondering, *does planning trips early just front-load the joy? Maybe I'd enjoy the trip itself more if I strip out the anticipation and book last minute.*

I think that view, though understandable, is ultimately misguided. The joy of travel is not zero-sum; there's not a finite amount of happiness you derive from a vacation, where any enjoyment before a trip takes away from the trip itself. In reality, planning early expands the overall amount of joy you get from a vacation and arguably helps you better appreciate the trip itself.

That's what happened when I found a $169 roundtrip flight between the United States and Japan and booked it ten months in advance. I had almost a year to look forward to the trip, read guides, watch Japanese shows, plan where I'd go and what I'd eat. When the trip finally came, I had an amazing time in Tokyo, of course. But that lasted a week. I got to enjoy the anticipation for ten months.

If planning trips well in advance is a useful tweak that makes us happier, why don't more of us do it? I have a few theories.

1. **We're lazy.** We have a trip we've been thinking of taking, but the planning process is intimidating: coordinating with travel partners, researching flights, booking accommodations. Like many stressful things in life, procrastination offers short-term relief.

2. **We're uninspired.** We'd like to go somewhere this summer, but where? It can be hard to plan a vacation if we're not sure where to visit.

3. **We're unsure when the best fare will pop up.** Without a good sense of when airfare is likely to go up or down, it can be difficult to plan the best time to book flights.

4. **We're scared of plans changing.** Most of us know what we're doing tomorrow. But what about six months from now? Or longer? People's plans change, and it can feel unsettling to lock yourself into a flight well in advance, especially considering how expensive it can be to reschedule or cancel them.

These are all valid concerns, so let's address them one by one.

1. **We're lazy.** Procrastination isn't priceless. There's no free lunch by waiting. Understanding that dawdling can rob you of both cheap flights and the joy of anticipation is motivation to plan earlier.

2. **We're uninspired.** Rather than approaching travel with the standard Destination First Method, use the Flight First Method. See where cheap flights pop up and wait for one that motivates you, either because it's an amazing price, an amazing destination, or ideally both.

3.   **We're unsure when the best fare will pop up.** There will always be some amount of uncertainty with flight prices. But just because they're volatile doesn't mean they're indecipherable. With an improved understanding of how airfare behaves from Chapter 7 and Goldilocks Windows for cheap flights from Chapter 4, and by employing the Flight First Method of booking, overpaying for flights will be a thing of the past.

4.   **We're scared of plans changing.** Schedules do change sometimes, but not *that* often. Ask yourself, are your plans actually likely to change, or are you just fearful of boxing in your future self? Travel at its core is about escape and exploration, so instead of viewing a far-out plane ticket as a possibly hindering commitment, think of it as an opportunity. Planners take more than twice as many vacation days as nonplanners, and they are much more likely to use that time off to travel, according to a poll from the U.S. Travel Association. By booking a flight and putting a vacation on your calendar, you're much more likely to actually take that trip than if you merely tell yourself maybe you'll do it when the time gets closer.

There's nothing inherently wrong with waiting to make travel plans. Not all trips can be planned ten months in advance. But it's important to recognize what we're giving up by waiting (happiness), what we're substituting (stress), and what the result often is (expensive flights).

THE SECOND BEST PART OF
TRAVEL IS MAKING MEMORIES

The 1997 study that found anticipation is the happiest part of travel made another surprising discovery as well.

In the experiment, researchers asked participants to rate their feelings about their vacation on a 7-point scale. Each traveler then repeated the survey at various points leading up to the trip, during, and after.

As we discussed, respondents in each of the three groups gave their highest marks before the trip. But their next highest response didn't come during the trip; it came after, when they were looking *back* on their travels. Rosy retrospection.

Take the survey responses of 21 people visiting Europe. A month prior, the respondents' feelings about the trip averaged 27.05. (Higher numbers indicate warmer feelings about the vacation.) Three days into the trip, the barometer had dropped to 24.38. At 8 days in it was virtually the same, 24.43. But when travelers filled out their survey on the flight home—the moment when we might assume feelings would be lower, with the impending end of a vacation and return to work—the average score showed a marked rise to 25.76. Three weeks later it remained at a higher level than it ever reached during the trip, 25.57.

Feelings about the trip took on a U-shape. The warmest sentiments came before and after the trip, not during. The worst part of traveling, it seems, is the trip itself. It's not that we don't enjoy trips, we just seem to enjoy the before and after even more.

If this cuts against the way you think about enjoying traveling, you're not alone. A (admittedly nonscientific) Twitter poll

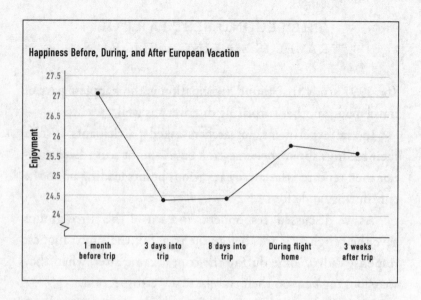

Happiness Before, During, and After European Vacation

of 805 Scott's Cheap Flights followers found that 60 percent of respondents said they enjoyed the trip itself most, followed by 23 percent the memories and 17 percent the anticipation. The way we think we enjoy traveling is precisely backward, in other words, from the way we actually do.

Why do we tend to enjoy traveling less than we enjoy the anticipation and the memories?

In part, it's a self-fulfilling prophecy. It's not just that we exhibit rosy prospection before a trip and rosy retrospection afterward. As important, the researchers noted, there is a "consistency effect: people align their memories of an event with their expectations held prior to the event." How much we *think* we'll enjoy a trip helps determine how much we *remember* enjoying the trip, regardless of our actual trip experience.

It also may be because while trips are finite, memories are endless. "Vacations continue to provide hedonic benefits even after they've long since passed because they live on in the stories we tell," Dr. Amit Kumar, an assistant professor of marketing and psychology at the University of Texas, told *New York Magazine*. Although the immediate afterglow of a trip may fade, travel memories persist as a fount of joy for the rest of your life. When you're watching Netflix and there's a scene in a Parisian café, it activates your memory of that wonderful French vacation you took. Every time you see Machu Picchu on Instagram or hear a friend planning to visit the Fushimi Inari Shrine, you get to relive your trip. You're back there again.

It's also an expectations game. When we book a trip somewhere, we tend to not think about the little day-to-day inconveniences that can happen on the road. We anticipate the wonderful food and beautiful sights and exciting people, not the ongoing stress of navigating a foreign land in a foreign language. And when we look back, we think less of the angst standing in line for two hours and more of the awe-inspiring view atop the Eiffel Tower.

There were a few of those notable mishaps during Cameron Burke's vacation to southern France. Cameron, an accountant in Denver, was so thrilled to see $460 roundtrip fares that he brought his mom and grandma along. During the vacation itself, though, his grandmother caught a cold in Barcelona, and at one point Cameron dinged the rental car backing out of a parking garage. "I had a couple of choice four-letter words when I scraped it up," he recalled. It was a pricey repair.

In retrospect, though, Cameron said it doesn't feel nearly as bad as it did at the time. "Looking back, I got a bill in the mail, we paid it, it was fine," he said.

This is a phenomenon known as Fading Affect Bias, the tendency of negative experiences to lose their salience over time. As we discussed about travel and regrets, things that felt horrendous in the moment feel not so bad later on. Sometimes stressful experiences even lead to positive memories, as you laugh in retrospect about that missed flight or crummy hotel. Time heals most wounds.

We also tend to remember trips not as the average of our feelings throughout but, instead, how we felt at both the most vivid and final moments. This is known as the Peak-End Rule. Not every moment of travel is fun or relaxing. If you were to ask a vacationer in Kenya who's sweaty or bored or hangry how they feel about their trip, their rating will likely be lower than if you ask them a year later, when their most intense memory is seeing a wild giraffe up close.

Professor Kahneman, whose research we discussed earlier, contends that the best way to understand the Peak-End Rule is by distinguishing between our Experiencing Self and Remembering Self. The Experiencing Self has a blast during the Lakers game taking in the arena's energy and watching LeBron show off, while the Remembering Self sees the entire experience as tainted because the team lost on a last-second shot.

"What defines a story are changes, significant moments, and endings," Kahneman said during a 2010 TED Talk. "Endings are very, very important." In fact, after Kahneman and his wife spent a memorable day vacationing in Switzerland, the couple actually cut their vacation short because they wanted the terrific day they'd just experienced to be the final one for their Remembering Selves. "That [way] we wouldn't ruin the memory," he said in an NPR interview.

Rather than the car or the cold, what do Cameron and his

family remember today? The views on the French Riviera, exploring Marseille's cathedrals, the food. Though it's been years since the trip, "If we're hanging out at a restaurant and mussels come out, we talk about the gigantic plate of mussels we got in the south of France," he said. Even his grandma, who got sick, remembers the trip fondly. "To this day, my grandmother keeps reminding me of the good time she had."

THE PERFECT VACATION, ACCORDING TO SCIENCE

Pulling together all our research on vacation and happiness, let's look at how to plan the perfect trip:

1. **Prioritize cheap flights.** Overpaying for airfare creates a sense of pressure and dread around the trip, corroding the joy of travel. Getting a good deal, on the other hand, adds salt to the entire experience, making each part of the trip more enjoyable. It's not just the financial windfall but also the mental freedom of knowing you did as well as you could buying your tickets.
2. **Take short trips.** Unless you're fortunate enough to have truly unlimited vacation time, you'll need to decide whether to parse your time into one big trip or multiple small ones. Trips around a week long are ideal for maximizing happiness; longer ones tend to have diminishing returns.
3. **Take more trips.** Three weeks of vacation and a $1,000 flight budget could get you one trip, or it could get you

three. Be savvy and opt for three. It's the small, frequent pleasures that do the most to boost our long-term happiness. Taking more trips also improves your vacation skill set by strengthening your ability to identify what parts of travel appeal to you personally. Plus, multiple trips a year give you more opportunities to test places further down your bucket list, rather than only sticking to crowded tourist favorites.

4. **Book your flights well in advance.** The time between booking a flight and taking that trip is the happiest part of travel. Anticipation is a powerful joy-inducer. By booking well in advance (as long as you get a great deal, of course), you extend the amount of time spent savoring the anticipation. Plus, booking flights in advance ensures you don't get stuck with expensive last-minute fares.

5. **If you're on the fence about a trip, say yes.** Studies show that in the long run, we tend to regret the things we *didn't* do. Even if a trip doesn't go as well as we'd hoped, the regret rarely lasts. What sticks with us is the interesting local cuisine we didn't try, the time we almost skydived but pulled out at the last minute, the far-flung trip we didn't take.

6. **Save something especially fun for the final day.** The last part of a trip has an outsized impact on our memory afterward. And the mental report that we concoct after a trip plays a huge role in shaping how we look back at it for years to come. By scheduling a particularly exciting activity on the last day of vacation—say, a big snorkel outing, or a romantic splurge dinner—you're helping improve your takeaway memories.

Happiness isn't an exact science. What works for most people doesn't necessarily jibe with any single individual. But we have plenty of research about which aspects of vacation and trip planning make most people happy and what stresses us out. We're led to believe that long trips and spontaneous last-minute bookings are best, when in reality it's short trips planned well in advance that do the most for our well-being. Embracing this science-backed approach to trip planning may not be intuitive, but I have no doubt it will make most of our vacations more enjoyable.

KEY TAKEAWAYS

- Vacationing isn't an inherent skill, but one that we improve with experience. Our tastes change over time; the only way to figure out what specific aspects of travel are personally meaningful is to travel more.
- We're far more likely to regret the trips we didn't take than the ones we did. Even bad moments on the road will soon evolve into funny memories.
- We get more enjoyment from anticipating a vacation than being on the trip itself. Planning vacations well in advance—rather than last-minute excursions—is an easy way to give yourself more joy (and get cheaper flights).
- We also tend to enjoy memories more than the trip itself. That's a feature, not a bug, because we get to relive a trip's highlights for much longer than we were actually on vacation.

12

PRO TIPS:
ADVANCED FLIGHT-BOOKING TACTICS
TO MAXIMIZE YOUR VACATION

WITH THE BASICS OF FLIGHT SEARCHING IN HAND AND A cheap flight mentality in mind, you're ready to start learning advanced methods for taking better vacations. These tips will range from adding extra destinations onto your trip to uncovering hidden flight options to finding mistake fares, the most sought-after treasure in the cheap flight world.

Think of these tactics not as a substitution for, but rather a complement to, the overarching strategy of prioritizing cheap flights.

GREEK ISLANDS TRICK

Nothing will kill your dreams of sunbathing in Santorini quicker than looking at flight prices to Santorini.

Pull up a flight search engine and see what fares look like

from your home airport to Santorini. From most U.S. airports they'll be anywhere between $1,500 and $5,000 roundtrip. Vile stuff. Who can afford that?

Before you give up hope of swimming in the Aegean Sea and admiring the impossibly white-and-blue Cycladic architecture, see if a nifty workaround can cut airfare to a fraction of its initial price: the Greek Islands Trick.

Say you live in the New York area. Flights from Newark to Santorini are typically around $1,500 roundtrip. Flights from Newark to Athens, meanwhile, are much, much cheaper. In August 2019, for example, they dropped to $294 roundtrip. And once you're that close to the Greek islands, flights from Athens to Santorini are regularly as low as $40 roundtrip.

If you only search for flights from New York to Santorini in a single itinerary, you can expect to pay $1,500. If you break your trip up into multiple itineraries, you could get to Santorini for $334 roundtrip. At that price you could bring your three closest friends along, cover their flights (what a mensch!), and *still* pay less than you would have without the Greek Islands Trick.

The Greek Islands Trick doesn't just work for flights to Greece. It can be useful for any remote destination where flights from the United States are expensive. Think Bali, Zanzibar, the Maldives. It doesn't even have to be somewhere remote; it can work going anywhere flights are expensive. For instance, flights from the United States to South Korea are typically over $1,000 roundtrip, but flights to Beijing are regularly under $400 roundtrip. Tack on flights from Beijing to Seoul for $200 roundtrip and you're still saving hundreds off normal flight prices.

The Greek Islands Trick

A normal booking to Santorini

Using the Greek Islands Trick

In late 2018, Thomas Potter, a Denver-based attorney, was relaxing at home around Thanksgiving and on a whim decided to check out what flights to Morocco would cost. Visiting Morocco had been a lifelong dream for Thomas—he'd even applied to join the Peace Corps there, but it didn't work out. With flights from Denver well over $1,000, though, justifying the cost of one ticket was tough, much less three more for his wife and two daughters. While poking around, however, he stumbled across flights from Rome to Rabat for $59 roundtrip. "Interesting," he thought, mentally filing it away.

Days later, he opened his inbox and got a jolt: Roundtrip flights from Denver to Rome had dropped all the way down to $346. Rome was certainly interesting, but Thomas had an epiphany. He could combine the $346 Rome flights with $59 Rabat flights, making the total cost of getting from Denver to Morocco just $405 roundtrip. He immediately rang up his wife. She knew about his Morocco dreams, but they'd always been unaffordable. Now? "All four of us were able to travel for the price of one," Thomas recounted.

Another benefit of the Greek Islands Trick that Thomas took advantage of: You can stagger your itinerary dates in order to spend as much time as you want in the first destination. (More on this strategy of building your own layovers shortly.) Thomas and his family were able to spend four days—including Easter Sunday—in Rome and Vatican City, which turned out to be the highlight of the trip for Thomas's wife.

Why does searching for flights from Denver to Rabat only show $1,000+ fares, whereas flights from Denver to Rome to Rabat are available for a combined $405? It's all because of the way airlines sell tickets. With rare exception, airlines will only let you book an itinerary that flies you on their planes or a partner airline. Not all airlines partner with one another; in fact, most airlines only partner with a handful of others, and some don't partner with any. You can't book a Delta flight that includes a segment on United, but you can book a Delta flight that includes a segment on KLM.

What this means in practice is that when you search for flights, say from Denver to Rabat, you'll see only routes on partner airlines, not any airline. For instance, the cheapest option at time of writing ($1,742 roundtrip) was Denver–Minneapolis–

Paris–Rabat, with the first two legs on Delta and the final leg on Air France.

If you're trying to get the best possible price, this is a problem. After all, the cheapest flights from Europe to Rabat are typically on a budget airline like Ryanair, like Thomas's $59 roundtrip tickets out of Rome. Those fares will never show up when searching from Denver to Rabat, however, because (at time of writing) Ryanair neither flies nor partners with any airline that flies to North America. Instead, a Denver–Rabat search will show you only allowable routes for the *entire* itinerary, like the $1,742 Delta–Air France option.

Think of it like you're buying a new iPhone and at checkout Apple offers you a choice of phone cases. Protecting your phone seems prudent, right? But Apple is only going to show you their expensive $40 cases at checkout, not the facsimile you can get on Amazon for $7.

So too with airlines. Delta's not going to tell you about a cheaper way to get to Rabat by pointing you toward Ryanair for the last leg. After all, Delta is in the business of maximizing Delta's profits. When it comes to finding cheap flights, you have to be your own best advocate.

Why are flights from Denver to Rabat so expensive? Think back to our discussion in Chapter 7 of how airfare is determined. It's not by the distance flown, and it's not the sum of the fares for each individual segment. Airfare is determined by demand and competition from the origin to the destination. Delta is one of the only airlines in the world that both flies out of Denver and has a partner (Air France) that flies into Rabat. With little competition, it charges high fares for anyone in Denver searching for flights to Rabat. Dozens of airlines fly from Denver to Europe, though, and more than half a dozen fly from Europe to Rabat. With fierce competition on those routes, fares get slashed much more frequently.

Think of it as though you were drafting professional athletes to compete in a pentathlon. LeBron James is the world's best at basketball, but if we also need him to compete in tennis and archery, he may be a liability. British Airways may have the cheapest fare from Denver to London, but its London–Rabat flight may be the most expensive.

The Greek Islands Trick doesn't mean you have to fly on budget airlines. When I got a $225 roundtrip flight to Brussels in 2012 and decided to tack on a trip to Dublin, the cheapest option was on Aer Lingus, not Ryanair. Finding the cheapest intra-European flights is no different from searching for domestic U.S. travel; whichever OTA or flight search engine you prefer will work just as well.

In fact, depending on your final destination, the last leg may work best on another mode of transportation altogether. Sometimes the cheapest route to Venice is a cheap flight to Milan paired with a two-hour train ride to Venice. Many islands in Greece are accessible from Athens by ferry. (The website Rome2rio is the easiest way to explore public transportation schedules and prices anywhere in the world, including trains, buses, and ferries.)

The Greek Islands Trick doesn't necessarily mean more layovers than booking a single itinerary. At time of writing, the cheapest flight from Newark to Santorini in early November was $1,907 roundtrip, with stops in Charlotte and Munich en route. Flights from Newark to Athens, meanwhile, were available nonstop for $485 roundtrip. Pair that with a separate

$40 flight from Athens to Santorini and you've got a $525 one-connection trip, rather than a $1,907 two-connection trip.

So how do you go about putting the Greek Islands Trick into practice for your particular trip?

Let's say you want to fly from Dallas to Dubrovnik. Flights from the United States to Croatia regularly exceed $1,300 roundtrip. Yikes! Too high! Instead of overpaying for a ticket like that, here's how to implement the Greek Islands Trick.

First, you'll need to work backward by figuring out the cheapest routes to Dubrovnik from elsewhere in Europe. To do this, pull up Google Flights, set DBV as your origin, and put Europe as your destination. Note that the resulting fares are of course *from* Dubrovnik, not *to* Dubrovnik, but this gives us an approximate sense of what fares to expect nevertheless.

Second, set the number of connections to nonstop. This step is optional, and if the initial results are more expensive than you hoped you can expand your search to include connecting flights, but I like to start with the best-case scenario and go from there. In this case, we see the cheapest nonstop flights from Dubrovnik are to London, Rome, and Zagreb.

FINDING NONSTOP ROUTES

Check the website Flightconnections.com to quickly and easily see all the nonstop flight options to or from any given airport.

(One note of caution: When trying to find the cheapest jump-off city to fly into, resist the temptation to look only at cities near your destination. In this Dubrovnik example, a flight to nearby Sofia [262 miles as the crow flies] costs $298 roundtrip with two connections and over eight hours of travel time, while a flight to London [1,061 miles] costs $75 roundtrip with no connections and under three hours of travel time. Don't assume nearby cities are always cheaper; use a tool like the fare map on Google Flights to check if major cities a bit farther away are actually cheaper and faster.)

Third, armed with the three cities we know are cheapest to reach from Dubrovnik, confirm that prices are in the same ballpark when reversing the route. In this case, starting in London brings the fare from $75 to $81 roundtrip, Rome decreases from $97 to $70 roundtrip, and Zagreb stays the same at $116 roundtrip. Given those cheap fares, we've confirmed that all three are plausible candidates for the Greek Islands Trick.

Sample Nonstop Roundtrip Fares From Dubrovnik

Fourth, check how fares are looking from Dallas to each of these gateway European cities. At time of writing, there are roundtrip flights in May to Zagreb for $1,176 (too high), London for $667 (decent), or Rome for $376 (excellent).

Even if there weren't cheap flights to any of these three cities in my initial search, those are the three I'd most keep my eyes on for future price drops. And if none of them see good price drops but I have my heart set on Croatia, I can always book a flight to wherever cheap pops up in Europe and then take a slightly pricier or less convenient flight onward to Dubrovnik.

Let's review our final options:

- Dallas–Dubrovnik (one itinerary) = $1,300 roundtrip
- Dallas–Zagreb ($1,176) + Zagreb–Dubrovnik ($116) = $1,292 roundtrip
- Dallas–London ($667) + London–Dubrovnik ($81) = $748 roundtrip
- Dallas–Rome ($376) + Rome–Dubrovnik ($70) = $446 roundtrip

Employing the Greek Islands Trick has brought fares to Croatia down from $1,300 to $446. Plus, you can space out your flights to spend as much time as you want in Rome before continuing onward to Dubrovnik. (Of course, if you'd prefer to visit London rather than Rome, there's nothing forcing you to go with the cheapest possible route here.) It's generally a good idea to schedule the flight to Dubrovnik at least a day after arriving in Rome to minimize the chances a delay or cancellation causes you to miss the onward flight.

Remember too that if you use the Greek Islands Trick and

break your trip into two itineraries, you don't have to book both flights at the same time. When $225 roundtrip flights to Belgium popped up, I booked them right away because I knew they wouldn't last long. I wasn't all that interested in spending time in Brussels, but I knew once I was in Europe it would be easy and cheap to hop elsewhere. So with $225 transatlantic flights secured, I spent the next few months researching where I might like to visit and looking at train prices and airfare before settling on a week in Ireland.

For Thomas, the best part of the Greek Islands Trick wasn't just visiting a country he'd always dreamed of seeing. It was watching how the trip transformed his young daughter and brought his blended family together. "Every room our baby went into she became the center of attention," he said. "She never changed back. She still waves at everyone who goes by because when we were traveling everyone engaged her in a way Americans typically don't. That trip changed her whole life."

BUILDING YOUR OWN LAYOVERS

A few years ago, my wife and I were looking into flights from Denver to Ukraine. With no nonstops available on that route, the cheapest option was a red-eye from Denver to Frankfurt, followed by a seven-hour layover before the flight onward to Kyiv.

At first glance that seemed like a horrible option. Who wants to spend seven hours in the Frankfurt Airport? At second glance, though, I realized it was an opportunity. I checked Rome2rio and confirmed that Frankfurt's airport train could get us downtown in ten minutes. Way better than killing time in the airport.

That's exactly what we ended up doing. We dropped our bags in airport luggage storage and hopped the train downtown. There was sausage from a delightful Mrs. Schreiber, apfelwein at a sidewalk café, even a pleasant nap in the park for our jet-lagged bodies. It was a lovely afternoon in a part of Germany we hadn't spent time in before.

Turning the trip into a two-for-one had a number of benefits. If we're flying all the way across an ocean, it's nice to see multiple places on the journey rather than just one city. Frankfurt isn't somewhere that had been on our radar, and the likelihood of us crossing the Atlantic to go there specifically was quite low. Much like a thirty-day trial of Netflix or a free sample of kombucha, this layover let us briefly check out the city and see if it's somewhere we'd want to come back and visit. (Spoiler: It is!) Best of all: It was free. We got to explore Frankfurt en route to Ukraine without having to pay anything extra.

Building your own layover is similar to the Greek Islands Trick in that the key is to cross the ocean as cheaply as possible. But rather than focusing on just reaching a remote destination as inexpensively as possible, building your own layover is a technique to add as many destinations to a trip as you want.

There are two primary ways to build your own layover. First, you can take advantage of a long layover in your flight itinerary, like we did in Frankfurt. (Most airlines will limit layovers to 24 hours or less.) This is a good option if an itinerary you're considering has a long layover somewhere interesting.

Some airlines and airports even offer perks for passengers with long layovers, including free hotels and tours. For example, depending on your flight schedule, airlines like Turkish, China Southern, and Royal Jordanian offer comped hotel rooms to passengers with long layovers. If you're flying through Seoul, Singapore, or Taipei, they offer free city tours for transiting passengers, and other airports like Doha offer highly discounted tours. The list of airlines and airports offering these perks changes regularly, so it's worth a quick Google search to see if it's an option for your trip.

However, the more versatile way to build your own layover is the Bookend Technique. If you want to visit a few cities, purchasing a single itinerary that includes all of them is liable to be expensive. Instead, the best approach is to just buy bookend flights—the outbound and return transoceanic flights—and leave the middle to book separately.

Let's walk through another personal example. In 2016, my wife and I were planning a trip from Denver to Southeast Asia, hoping to explore all around the region. Rather than booking all our flights in a single itinerary, though, we just booked the transpacific legs: an outbound flight from Denver to Hong Kong, then a return flight three weeks later from Seoul to Denver. It was critical for us to get the bookend flights booked at a good price because long flights can have a wide price range. So when we saw a cheap option we could buy with our frequent flyer miles, we booked it quickly because we knew it might not last long.

Conversely, we didn't have to worry about booking flights around Southeast Asia far in advance because the short routes and fierce competition meant fares wouldn't get exorbitant. Our one-way flight from Hong Kong to Borneo: $98. The next flight to Bali: $95. Onward to Singapore: $99. From there to Hanoi: $105. And on to our final stop in Seoul: $168. Total cost of flights to traipse around Southeast Asia for nearly a month: $565 per person.

If I had tried to book a single itinerary with all these stops, the total cost would've been in the thousands. That's because the cheapest airline on one route might be the most expensive on another, but a single search will show only options within one airline or one airline's partner network. Instead, we searched each route separately and booked the cheapest flights à la carte. These five flights within Southeast Asia ended up being on four different airlines (Trigana Air, Citilink, Tigerair, and Vietjet) none of which partner with one another or transpacific airlines.

The Bookend Technique also gave us time to research where we wanted to go. Even though we hadn't figured out where in Southeast Asia we planned to visit, having the bookends gave us a framework to fill out the middle of the trip. We could take our time planning where else to visit.

In general, the best way to implement the Bookend Technique is with an open-jaw flight. An open-jaw flight is when you fly into one city and back from another, like we did flying Denver–Hong Kong and returning Seoul–Denver. The benefit is straightforward: Open-jaw flights save you from having to backtrack. If we had booked a normal roundtrip flight into and out of Hong Kong, we would've needed to get an additional flight from Seoul to Hong Kong for our flight home. Open-jaws aren't worth it if they're substantially more expensive than a regular roundtrip, but in general, if roundtrip flights to City A and City B are similarly priced, an open-jaw flight into A and out of B is usually about the same price.

To summarize, here are a few best practices for building your own layovers: First, it's typically cheapest if you book the middle leg(s)—like our flights within Southeast Asia—separately, rather than including them in your transoceanic itinerary. Doing so allows you to get the cheapest connecting flight (or whatever mode of transportation), rather than only flights that are within the same airline or alliance you flew across the ocean.

Using an Open-Jaw Flight to See Two (or More) Cities

Second, if you're building a trip that has separate flight itineraries, it's ideal to space them out by at least a day or two. If your Cathay Pacific flight to Hong Kong is set to arrive at 10 a.m. and your AirAsia flight departs at 11:30 a.m., virtually any delay would cause you to miss the second flight, especially considering the time needed to clear immigration and customs. If you miss a connection on a single itinerary it's no big deal, the airline is still responsible for getting you rebooked to your final destination. But when you're talking about multiple itineraries, Cathay Pacific won't help you rebook your missed AirAsia flight. By building in a buffer day or two, you minimize your chance of a missed flight and give yourself time to check out another city en route.

There are a few airlines that offer free stopover programs when transiting their hub. Icelandair, for example, offers travelers flying to Europe a free stop in Reykjavík up to 7 days at no additional expense. A few other airlines do so as well, including TAP (up to 5 days in Portugal), Finnair (up to 5 days in Finland), Qatar Airways (up to 2 days in Doha), and All Nippon Airways (up to a week in Japan, typically for about $100 extra). But in general, it tends to be significantly less expensive and more flexible to build your own layover.

USING THE 24-HOUR RULE TO YOUR ADVANTAGE

Think back to the 24-hour rule, that federal regulation requiring airlines to let customers cancel tickets they booked directly as long as they do so within 24 hours of purchase. While it may seem straightforward, there are three scenarios in which it can be a traveler's secret weapon.

First, remember that airlines normally charge exorbitant cancellation fees on all but the most expensive tickets. If you want to cancel a domestic ticket, most airlines will charge $200 to do so. Canceling international flights can run $400 or more. And if you bought a basic economy ticket, most airlines won't let you cancel your ticket for any fee. The exception, of course, is if you cancel within 24 hours of booking. Even basic economy tickets are eligible for the 24-hour rule refund.

The fact that refunds are normally so expensive underscores the second reason this rule is so beneficial: It gives you time to consider a great fare that you're not 100 percent sure you want to buy.

When my friend Dan got an email about $230 roundtrip flights from Washington, DC, to Dublin, he knew that fare wouldn't last very long. The problem? His wife, Nadia, was stuck in a work meeting all afternoon. Dan knew he had two options. He could wait until that evening when his wife got home and book their flights then, but in all likelihood a fare that good would be gone by then. The second option: Take his best guess about which week would work well for both their schedules and book it. By going with the latter option, Dan locked in the fare for 24 hours, giving them time to decide if they wanted to keep the tickets or get a full refund.

It was quite the "Honey, I'm home!" moment when Nadia walked in the door and Dan asked if she wanted to visit Ireland for $230 apiece. She looked at her schedule, and the week in May that Dan had picked did indeed work on her end. She confirmed with her boss first thing the next morning that taking a week off in mid-May would work. After all, if her boss rejected the request, it was important to know before the 24 hours were up and the refund window closed. Luckily the request was approved, on the condition that Nadia notify her boss next time there's another cheap flight.

If Dan had wanted to be even more next level, he could have booked multiple flights and given Nadia an option of various weeks to choose from. Perhaps one week in March, one in April, and another in May. They could have chosen which one to keep, then gotten refunds on the other two.

One of the most memorable misses in my flight-hunting career was a time I brazenly ignored my own advice. I was up late poking around Google Flights (as one does) and found flights departing the United States to India for $180 roundtrip. I pinged my friend Lee to see if he wanted to go. It was not a difficult sell. But rather than book immediately, we spent the next two hours researching when and where in India to go. We finally settled on flying into Mumbai and out of Delhi in early March to be there for the spring Holi festival. As I entered my payment information and clicked to book, I got an error message: "Your fare is no longer available." I'd taken too long and missed the boat. As Lee said, "We waffled."

If we had booked flights right away (and ideally multiple trip options) we would have locked in the fare, given ourselves 24 hours to research traveling in India, and been able to make a go or no-go decision the next day. Instead, we waited too long and wound up with a forlorn memory of the India trip that almost was.

The third reason the 24-hour rule is so powerful is it lets you switch if a better flight pops up soon after booking.

On the evening of May 16, 2019, Scott's Cheap Flights members across the country, from New York to Denver to Seattle and elsewhere, were alerted to cheap Vietnam flights that had just popped up. One of those who jumped on the deal was Donald Garrett, a Washington, DC–based educator. He'd never been to Vietnam before, and $572 to Ho Chi Minh City was a great price. Why not go?

The next morning, Donald got another email: Fares to Tokyo had just gone on sale. "I was much more interested in Japan," he said. Though DC wasn't one of the cheap departure cities initially, flights from Richmond to Tokyo were available for $696 roundtrip, far less than normal. "Richmond is only an hour and a half away from where I live, and I have family there. So what's a quick car ride or cheap train ride for a 60 percent discount?" He booked the Tokyo flight and then, because it had been less than 24 hours, proceeded to cancel the Vietnam ticket for a full refund.

As luck would have it, a few hours later Donald got yet another email: Prices to Tokyo had not only dropped further, but they were now available out of DC. Donald took advantage of the 24-hour rule once again, canceling his Richmond flight and booking from DC to Tokyo for just $584 roundtrip. "An amazing deal," Donald said. "And no extra train or car travel required."

As we explored in Chapter 7, it's not uncommon for airlines to get into fare wars with one another, dropping prices tit-for-tat often in the span of a few hours. When this happens, the 24-hour rule lets already-booked passengers get an even better deal, whether it's a lower fare, a better routing, or both.

If a deal you've bought gets cheaper within 24 hours of purchase, it's important to book your new flight *before* canceling your old one.

To understand why, let's use Ned as an example. Ned booked a $440 connecting flight from Los Angeles to Paris on American. The next morning, Delta responds by offering $350 nonstop flights on the same route. He's thrilled to get a cheaper fare and better route, so he hurriedly cancels his $440 American flight. As he goes to book the new $350 flight, Delta suddenly doubles the fare. Ned scrambles to rebook his original American flight, but that fare has now also gone up to $700. (After all, airfare is highly volatile and always changing.) Instead of a $440 connecting flight to France or a $350 nonstop flight, Ned has no flight. Once you cancel a flight, there are no takebacks.

One simple trick would have ensured Ned didn't wind up in this position: booking the new flight first, then canceling the old one. If he had booked the $350 Delta flight before he canceled the $440 American one, the worst-case scenario is he barely misses the 24-hour window to cancel the American flight. But rather than being stuck with two flights, Ned could instead cancel the nonstop Delta flight he just booked and be no worse off than he was yesterday when he excitedly bought a cheap trip to Paris.

Understanding the 24-hour rule opens up a ton of options for booking cheap fares and improving flights you've already purchased. But where the 24-hour rule is especially crucial is when you encounter the holy grail of cheap flights: a mistake fare.

MISTAKE FARES

It didn't matter that he'd never thought about visiting Croatia, or that he hadn't cleared the vacation request with his boss.

All that mattered when Josh Samuels opened the email was that flights from his home in Columbus, Ohio, to the Croatian capital, Zagreb—normally over $2,000—were inexplicably available for $350 roundtrip.

Josh and his wife had experienced a number of recent trag-
edies in their personal lives that year. "We really wanted to get
away for a bit and clear our heads," he said. When that incredibly cheap deal to Croatia hit his inbox, it seemed like fate. "We
saw it and immediately booked. It was exactly what we needed
given the circumstances."

This was no normal deal that Josh and his wife booked. It
was the crown jewel of the cheap flights world: a mistake fare.

A mistake fare is when an airline accidentally sells a flight
at a cartoonishly low price. Think New York City to Milan for
$130 roundtrip, San Jose to Osaka for $169 roundtrip, or $225
roundtrip from Washington, DC, to Brussels. These are all
deals I've personally booked.

A number of factors can cause a mistake fare, including:

Human error: When a roundtrip flight to Europe accidentally
gets priced at $130, the most likely culprit is someone at the air-
line meant to price it at $1,300 and forgot the last zero.

Technological mistake: American Airlines and its partners
currently fly to over a thousand cities. The number of possible
origin-destination pairs from a thousand cities is nearly half a
million. Once you add in twelve months of possible dates and
dozens of different fare classes and routes for each pair, the number of different flights you could currently book through American is many, many millions. And that's just American; there are
hundreds of other airlines around the world. It'd be impossible to price each of those routes individually, so airlines turn to
complex pricing algorithms. On occasion, these algorithms will
churn out a price for a given route that's far lower than intended.

Partner miscommunication: Delta isn't the only seller of Delta tickets. You can buy them on partner airlines like Air France, booking sites like Orbitz or Expedia, even old-school brick-and-mortar travel agencies. Sometimes information about a specific sale, discount, or fee will get bungled in transit.

Foreign currency devaluation: In 2012, Myanmar's government stopped pegging their currency, the kyat, to the U.S. dollar. Virtually overnight, it shifted from 6 kyat per $1 to 800 kyat per $1. As a result, travelers were able to book $259 flights in business or first class out of Yangon, tickets that had previously cost well over $10,000.

Abrupt schedule changes: Airlines did major surgery on their schedules in the wake of the 2020 coronavirus pandemic, and one byproduct of all that flux was a surge in the number of mistake fares. In the span of one week, Scott's Cheap Flights found four different mistake fares, including $210 roundtrip from Los Angeles to Chile and $290 roundtrip from New York City to Brazil, both nonstop.

"Intentional" mistakes: Every so often, an airline will "misprice" a flight as a PR stunt. According to industry expert Gary Leff, now-defunct Independence Air once loaded "mistake fares" onto their website and alerted local reporters in an attempt to generate publicity. Though these weren't genuine error fares, the result was incredibly cheap tickets all the same.

When you come across an error fare, the most important thing is to act quickly. Remember the Hotcakes Principle: The better the fare, the shorter it's going to last. Mistake fares are the best of the best, and airlines will race to fix them as quickly as they can, so their lifespan rarely exceeds six hours. They could disappear any minute—like that $180 roundtrip flight from the United States to India that I just missed out on.

If you're wondering whether the airlines can retroactively charge you the full ticket amount, the answer is emphatically no. Take it from the Department of Transportation: "After a ticket is fully purchased—with either money or points—and the transaction is completed, the airline is prohibited from increasing the price of the ticket or requiring the passenger to pay additional money unless the airline provided notice to the consumer of the potential for an increase in a government imposed tax or fee and obtained the consumer's consent."

What if you find a mistake fare but you're not 100 percent sure about when or where to go? I recommend booking quickly and remembering the handy 24-hour rule we just discussed. Mistake fares by nature don't last long, and the more time you spend researching and deciding, the more you risk the deal disappearing. Because of the 24-hour rule, booking quickly just locks in the price. Think of it as a free day to decide if you want to keep the flight or cancel it for a full refund.

But Scott, if these prices are a mistake, will airlines actually honor them?

I've been watching mistake fares for the better part of a decade, and in the vast majority of cases, airlines choose to honor them. For years, they did so because a Department of Transportation regulation required airlines to honor all tickets booked through their website. When that regulation was undone in 2015, many expected that airlines would never again honor error fares.

Those fears have not come to fruition. Instead, airlines continue to honor most mistake fares (think 90 percent or so) not because they have to, but because they want to. It's a smart business decision.

Take a recent example. In 2018, Hong Kong Airlines put normally $5,000 business class flights from California to all over Southeast Asia on sale for as low as $560 roundtrip. By the time the mistake was fixed a few hours later, thousands of people had booked flights to Bali, Bangkok, and Ho Chi Minh City.

Hong Kong Airlines had a choice. They could cancel thousands of tickets and face an irate backlash on social media and in the press. The airline's reputation would take a huge hit among everyone who had their deal of a lifetime taken away (plus all those people's social media followers). Social media uproars like these aren't trivial; they can result in a significant financial impact for the company. In the days after passenger David Dao was bloodied up being dragged off an overbooked airplane in 2017, United Airlines' market cap dropped $1 billion amidst a public backlash.

Rather than canceling people's tickets, Hong Kong Airlines opted to honor them. In doing so, the airline generated a massive amount of positive press coverage. Yes, they lost a nontrivial amount of potential revenue by selling business class seats at 90 percent off normal prices. But the boost to brand equity was sweeping. Airline marketing departments would pay millions for the number of glowing articles written about Hong Kong Airlines that week, not to mention thousands of exuberant social media posts. The airline even lemons-to-lemonaded the situation, handing out postcards on board to "the lucky few to get that deal of a lifetime" and encouraging them to post photos of their trip on social media with an #hkairlines hashtag.

Similarly, when Cathay Pacific accidentally sold $16,000 business class flights from Vietnam to New York for $675 to kick off 2019, they tweeted the next day: "Happy 2019 all, and to those who bought our good—VERY good surprise 'special' on New Year's Day, yes—we made a mistake but we look forward to welcoming you on board with your ticket issued. Hope this will make your 2019 'special' too! #promisemadepromisekept #lessonlearnt."

In rare cases, an airline may decide not to honor a mistake fare. According to the Department of Transportation, "airlines may cancel any reservations booked at the mistaken fare price, but airlines are required to reimburse consumers for the full ticket price, all optional services purchased, and any reasonable, actual, and verifiable out-of-pocket expenses that were made in reliance upon the ticket purchase (for example, nonrefundable hotel or rental car reservations)." It stinks to have your hopes dashed, but the good news is you'll never be worse off than before you booked the deal, and in the vast majority of cases, you'll end up with an unbelievably cheap ticket.

How do you know if an airline has honored a mistake fare? In some high-profile cases the airline will announce on Twitter or elsewhere that they're honoring it, but a public pronouncement doesn't always happen. Instead, it's often a no-news-is-good-news situation. When an airline cancels a ticket, they'll email you, almost always within a few days of the mistake. To be safe, I recommend waiting two weeks after you've received an e-ticket number (which indicates that your ticket has been issued). If the ticket hasn't been canceled by that point, you can be confident the mistake was honored and get busy planning your trip.

Given their unpredictable nature and brief lifespan, there's no foolproof way to find mistake fares. Think of it like trekking through the Himalayas, hoping to see a snow leopard. The more time you spend looking, the better your odds, but even then it's still quite rare.

There are two factors that can help. First, error fares tend to happen more on nights, weekends, and holidays. The $130 Milan flight I found was on a Saturday night; the $675 business class flight out of Vietnam was on New Year's; flights from the United States to Abu Dhabi for $220 roundtrip popped up on Christmas morning. The reason is that these are times when few staff are in the airline's office, so a mistake is less likely to be caught.

Second, discovering mistake fares is what services like Scott's Cheap Flights are there for. Unless you particularly love spending your free time hunting for these rare gems, letting experts do it for you is the best way to ensure you won't miss the next amazing deal.

For Josh Samuels, booking the mistake fare to Croatia was all about being opportunistic and embracing serendipity. "Never in our life had we thought about visiting Croatia," he said. And if they had, they probably would have gone to the tourist-favorite Dalmatian Coast, he conceded. Were it not for an unexpected deal like that, "I don't think central Croatia would've ever been in our plans. But I'm so excited it was because it was such a great experience." Hiking around Plitvice Lakes National Park was a hidden gem for the couple, as was taking the train over to the Swiss Alps. "We already want to go back!" he said.

A few weeks after booking the deal, as they were eagerly planning the trip, Josh and his wife were curious to see what flights from Columbus to Zagreb normally cost. They pulled up the exact same flight and gasped: $2,200. Taking advantage of the $350 mistake fare had saved them a collective $3,700. "It was one of those 'Oh shit, we actually did this!' moments," Josh said. "The rush of being able to lock down that deal was incredible."

LAST-MINUTE FLIGHTS

What do grocery stores often do with items nearing the end of their shelf life? Put them in the discount bin. After all, once an item passes its expiration date, it's no longer sellable and it goes to waste. If something is about to spoil, getting any amount of money is a victory, so a discount ("priced to sell!") makes perfect sense.

Flights have expiration dates of their own: the minute a plane door closes. At that point, each empty seat generates exactly $0 in revenue. The logical strategy would be to discount prices the closer an unfilled seat gets to its expiration date, right?

For years, this was the approach airlines took. Airlines had had a long-standing practice of putting unsold seats "on sale at the last minute in an effort to fill up the plane," according to a 1987 *New York Times* article. But with airlines like People Express, which tried to avoid "spoilage" at all costs, increasingly going out of business because they weren't generating enough revenue selling tickets, the pricing strategy began to change.

Nowadays the practice of slashing last-minute fares has become virtually extinct. Not only that, it has been replaced by its polar opposite: jacking up last-minute fares. What happened?

Airlines took a close look at who was buying fares in the last week or two before a flight. Turns out it wasn't the typical leisure travelers. Sure, a handful of twenty-somethings would show up at the airport and book a discounted flight to somewhere unexpected, but most vacationers preferred to book their trips months in advance.

Instead, the people commonly booking last-minute flights were business travelers. After all, their schedules are constantly changing, such that it's often impossible to make travel plans more than a week or two out.

NEGOTIATING FOR MORE WHEN A FLIGHT IS OVERSOLD

If you've got some flexibility in your schedule, volunteering to get bumped can be a big windfall. I've gotten $900 when an airline oversold the flight I was on, and a colleague of mine a couple of years ago got $10,000 for giving up her seat. If the airline asks for volunteers and you're interested, the key is to know that *everything* is negotiable. For instance, they may offer $200 initially, but you can tell them you're only interested if it gets to $500. Or if they need multiple volunteers, say you're willing but you want the same compensation they offer the highest bidder.

It's not just the amount of money. You can ask for other perks as well, like meal vouchers, hotel vouchers, access to lounges, a better routing on your replacement flight, even business class. They'll rarely mention these possibilities explicitly, but like In-N-Out Burger, there's a secret menu. You won't always be granted a business class upgrade for asking, but you'll rarely be offered if you don't ask. The airline's willingness to negotiate depends on how desperate they are for volunteers.

Why does it matter that business travelers are much more likely to book last-minute flights than leisure travelers? Think back to the charts in Chapter 7 of how the two groups of travelers behave. Leisure travelers are price-sensitive—they care a lot about the cost. Business travelers, meanwhile, are price-insensitive because it doesn't matter to them what the fare costs. Why should they care when their companies are footing the bill?

It dawned on the airlines that they'd been doing it all wrong. Instead of pursuing the goal of filling all seats, the airlines concluded, they ought to pursue the goal of maximal profits.

Rather than slashing prices on unsold seats nearing their expiration date, airlines began *raising* prices in order to generate as much revenue as possible from business travelers. If they could get a single businessperson to spend $1,000 for a ticket, that was worth more than nine leisure travelers buying tickets at $100 each. (All things equal, those nine passengers may also be less valuable to the airline than one passenger because they entail marginally higher costs, from drinks to service to higher fuel needs.)

It's not that airlines wouldn't like for their planes to be full; it's that filling capacity is not the same as maximizing profit. Money is more important to airlines than full planes. Allowing some number of seats to spoil is necessary in order to shake down business travelers, otherwise companies could hold out until the last minute to book and end up paying far less than they'd otherwise be willing to.

The same dynamic is behind why standby fares—discounted tickets for the next available open seat on an airline—have all but disappeared. A cheap last-minute option would undermine an airline's ability to gouge business travelers.

There is one category of airline where you can still frequently find last-minute deals: budget carriers. Few business travelers fly on airlines like Spirit and Frontier, which cater primarily to vacationers. Even if you primarily avoid flying budget airlines, should you find yourself needing a last-minute flight, you may find the savings enough to warrant an exception. In addition, routes that are more oriented toward leisure travelers are less likely to see the extreme last-minute price hikes. Last-minute flights to Hawaii won't typically see the type of price jump that last-minute flights to London might.

HIDDEN-CITY TICKETING

As we discussed in Chapter 7, airfare pricing depends on dozens of elements. Contrary to popular perception, how far you fly is a relatively unimportant factor. After all, connecting flights are usually cheaper than nonstop ones, even though you fly more miles with a connecting flight. Travelers prefer shorter itineraries and are willing to pay more for them.

Let's walk through an example: one-way flights from Orlando to Newark. United Airlines Flight 2032 flies that route nonstop on December 7 for, at time of writing, $121. Meanwhile, United Airlines also offers fares from Orlando to Richmond, via Newark, for $88. The $88 fare includes a seat on United Flight 2032.

In other words, you can buy a flight to Newark for $121, or the same flight to Newark *plus* a flight to Richmond for $88. A cheap flight aficionado would buy the $88 ticket and just skip the Newark–Richmond leg.

This tactic is called hidden-city ticketing, and it can save hundreds on airfare.

Hidden-City Ticketing

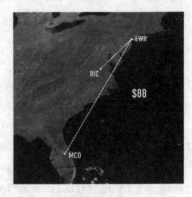

How is it possible that a flight from Orlando to Newark gets significantly cheaper by tacking on an additional leg to Richmond? It's because airlines view the two itineraries very differently. Flights to Newark are in high demand among business travelers who don't care what the fare is. And passengers of all stripes are willing to pay a premium for nonstop flights. Flights to Richmond, meanwhile, are not nearly as popular, and that's especially true for connecting flights. With little demand, United offers lower fares on that route.

While the benefit of hidden-city ticketing is clear (cheaper flights), it's important to be mindful of the risks. Airlines forbid the practice in their fine print because it undermines their ability to set different prices for different routes. Though few in number, there still exist travelers who get caught by the airline (typically because they bought an extraordinary number of hidden-city tickets). In those instances, airlines have been known to bar the passenger from their onward flight or even strip them of frequent flyer miles.

That said, it's important to note that hidden-city ticketing is neither illegal nor immoral. No law is broken when a passenger decides not to take a flight he or she bought. Though airlines have twice sued to crack down on hidden-city ticketing, in both cases, the lawsuits were dismissed. There's a reason the *New York Times'* Ethicist gave his seal of approval to hidden-city ticketing: When consumers buy something, they're under no obligation to use the entire product. This is true whether it's a plane ticket or an extra-large pizza.

Given their concealed nature, hidden-city tickets can be hard to find. Rather than spending hours testing various routes looking for a cheaper fare, there's a flight search engine, Skiplagged, that does the legwork for you. Unlike other OTAs, Skiplagged specializes in finding discounted hidden-city tickets.

In general, you'll only find cheaper hidden-city ticket fares if you're traveling to a hub city. That's because most airlines operate a hub-and-spoke route model, whereby the majority of their flights are to or from a central city. Think Atlanta (Delta), Philadelphia (American), or Denver (United). If you want to visit a major hub city like Chicago, chances are good there's a cheaper hidden-city ticket. If you want to visit a small nonhub city like

Birmingham, it's highly unlikely there'll be a cheaper hidden-city ticket.

If you find a cheap hidden-city ticket that interests you, there are a few precautions to keep in mind. First, don't tell the airline or gate agent about your plans, lest they cancel your ticket. It's highly unlikely the airline would find out on their own, especially if you're not constantly buying hidden-city tickets.

Second, don't check a bag. Remember, bags get checked to your itinerary's final destination (Richmond in the opening example), not your connecting city (Newark).

Third, hidden-city ticketing only works on a one-way flight or the final leg of a roundtrip flight. The reason why: If you skip a leg of your itinerary, airlines will automatically cancel all remaining flights on that itinerary. Assuming you need to fly roundtrip, booking two separate one-ways (even if it's on the same airline) is an easy workaround, because after you skip the Newark–Richmond leg, for instance, there wouldn't be any flights left on your outbound itinerary for the airline to cancel. Similarly, if you booked an itinerary that took you Orlando–Newark–Orlando–Miami, you could ditch the final Orlando–Miami leg because you wouldn't have any subsequent flights to worry about getting canceled.

Given the complexities, hidden-city ticketing isn't for beginners. But if you're comfortable with it, as I am, it can be another great tool in your arsenal to find cheap flights.

THE SURPRISING BEST WEEK
FOR INTERNATIONAL TRAVEL

Growing up, Lance Stack hadn't gone overseas much. Neither had his wife. In their twenties, they fell in love with each other, and then with traveling the world.

While many around them were settling down and having kids, as newlyweds Lance and his wife had other priorities. After taking their first trip to England, they were smitten. "Neither of us had traveled much, and then all of a sudden we got a taste of it and just couldn't get enough of it," he explained. Over the better part of a decade, they traveled to thirty different countries, from Iceland to New Zealand to Greece.

"Then we had kids and that all kind of stopped," Lance recounted from his home in Hot Springs, Arkansas. When they first had twin boys, and then a baby girl a few years later, it seemed like their travel days were over. And for a while, they were.

Traveling internationally with kids is difficult for many reasons. It's a practical challenge to pack all the kids' things, get the family to the airport, stave off a midflight meltdown, and organize logistics once you arrive. It's a financial challenge, buying airfare (not to mention everything else) for five instead of two. And it's a scheduling challenge, trying to work around the kids' school breaks.

Of these challenges, it's scheduling that is the least flexible. There are only a few big breaks throughout the school year, and as we discussed in Chapter 4, summer and Christmastime are two of the most difficult times of year to get a cheap flight.

There's one week of the year, though, that's a hidden gem for international travel: Thanksgiving. Most kids are out of school for at least a five-day weekend if not the entire week. Ditto for most adults at their jobs, so few if any vacation days are required for Thanksgiving trips.

But Scott, I thought traveling over Thanksgiving was expensive as hell. My flights home are always double what they normally cost.

True! Thanksgiving is one of the most expensive times of the year to fly *domestically*. When millions of Americans travel home on the same day, the result, unsurprisingly, is exorbitant fares. In fact, a 2017 poll of Americans found that, aside from Christmas, Thanksgiving was viewed as the holiday with the worst air travel hassles.

Here's the catch, though: While there's a surge in demand for domestic flights, there's no similar uptick for international flights. In fact, according to data from the Bureau of Transportation Statistics, November is consistently one of the *least* popular months to travel internationally.

That's why Thanksgiving is a diamond in the rough for cheap flights. While most Americans are jockeying for expensive domestic flights, cheap flight aficionados are booking underpriced international flights.

Take Eric Lee, a 24-year-old Bay Area resident working in education tech. "I wasn't going to go home to visit family for Thanksgiving because domestic flights had gotten too expensive," he said. But when he got an email alert that fares from San Jose to Beijing had dropped to $294 roundtrip, his Thanksgiving plans changed. Instead of paying $600 or more to fly home to Missouri, Eric spent under $300 and got to spend the week with extended family in China. "Looks like I lucked out!"

Taking advantage of the Thanksgiving loophole doesn't mean having to leave your family in the lurch. When fares from Charlotte to Montreal dropped to $243 roundtrip, Allison Folger managed to book six tickets before prices jumped back up. "Sending the whole family to Canada for Thanksgiving!" she emailed.

For Lance Stack and his family, two obstacles prevented them from traveling more: finding time and finding a deal. With three young kids and a wife who worked as an elementary school principal, traveling outside of scheduled breaks was a nonstarter, but during Christmas and summer, all the fares he saw were preposterous. Though the family had time off every Thanksgiving, they usually spent it hosting family and eating turkey.

That had been the default plan for Thanksgiving 2019, until an unexpected email hit Lance's inbox on May 30 about flights to Rome for $300 roundtrip on Delta.

"When that popped up, I thought Italy would be a great place to take the kids," Lance said. "When I looked at the dates, I figured I'm going to look at Thanksgiving break because the kids are off school. Lo and behold, it turned out we can go over Thanksgiving break."

Lance knew that a fare this good wasn't liable to last long. His wife was in a meeting at work, something he normally wouldn't interrupt, but $300 flights to Europe deserve an exception. So rather than risk waiting until she got home, Lance called her.

"Hey, want to go to Italy over Thanksgiving?" he asked.

"What?"

"That thing I signed up for, Scott's Cheap Flights. We can all go for $1,500."

"Umm, yeah! Let me check on a couple of things."

"Okay, but don't dillydally. I don't think these'll last forever."

Two hours later, the Stack family had five tickets from Dallas to Rome. Though the airport in Little Rock was closer to home, fares from there were at least quadruple the price. By being flexible about which airport they departed from, a strategy discussed at greater length in Chapter 4, Lance and his family saved $5,000 for the price of a four-hour drive to Dallas.

Their kids, meanwhile, were beside themselves with excitement to explore the Colosseum, Venice's canals, and of course gelato. The parents were excited to see Italy through the eyes of their kids, and to do so without shredding the family budget. "This is a game changer for us, to be able to know that we can go to Europe for $1,500," Lance said. "I'd figured on shelling out $6,000 for it."

As for the family they usually see over Thanksgiving? Lance broke the news apologetically that they couldn't share turkey this year. "We're going to be in Italy."

USING CREDIT CARD POINTS

It's Thursday evening. You're sitting at your computer, glass of red wine in hand, when you stumble across a screamer of a deal to Vietnam: $430 roundtrip with a single connection in Tokyo.

Your heart drums. Sweat beads on your brow. Your chest tightens as you go from disbelief ("Is this fare real?") to acceptance ("It's real and it's spectacular.") to embrace ("I am about to become the type of person who visits Vietnam for $430 roundtrip.").

But as you pull out your credit card to pay, you remember about that pile of points you've got stashed away. Should you pay with those instead?

It's a tricky question that depends on a number of factors. There's not a permanently correct answer—"Always pay with points!" or "Never pay with points!"—so let's explore the various considerations you should weigh before deciding how to buy your flight.

Following the generally accepted parlance, I'll refer to "miles" as frequent flyer miles that are associated with a particular airline, and "points" as credit card points associated with a particular bank or credit card company. You get miles after flying on Delta, and you get points after making a purchase on your American Express card.

How Miles Work

Virtually every airline in the world has a frequent flyer mileage program. Once you get enough miles, you can redeem them for free flights (including on partner airlines), upgrades, or other perks.

The number of miles required for a free flight has traditionally varied by region but not by city. For example, even though a flight from Chicago to Barcelona might cost $500 and a flight from Fargo to Barcelona might cost $1,200, each would cost 60,000 miles roundtrip. Though redemptions were flat rate, award availability varied. Blackout dates around the holidays were common, for instance, while availability was plentiful in January.

Increasingly, though, mileage redemption costs are becoming variable. Just like cash fares went from one-size-fits-all decades ago to highly volatile today, so too are award flights undergoing a similar transformation. The number of miles required used to be independent of the cash price for the same flight, but that's becoming less and less the case. For instance, on a date when flights from Chicago to Barcelona cost $800 roundtrip, an award flight might require 80,000 miles, while a date when that route costs $450 might run 60,000 miles.

The simplest way to determine how much value you're getting from your miles is to compare the miles amount to the cash price. A flight that costs 60,000 miles or $1,200 gets you a decent 2 cents per point in value (1,200 / 60,000 = 0.02), while a 60,000 mile or $450 flight gets you just 0.75 cents per point in value.

Given the complex nature of airline miles, there are a few pieces of background knowledge that are important to be cognizant of:

Miles are not the same between programs. A Delta mile is not equivalent to a United mile, just like a U.S. dollar is not equivalent to an Australian dollar. There are fierce disputes about which miles are worth the most, but there's no objective measure of value.

You can't transfer miles between programs. You can't convert United miles into Lufthansa miles, American miles, or any other miles. But . . .

You can redeem miles for flights on partner airlines. This is critical to understand. You can redeem United miles for a Lufthansa flight, just as you can with American and Japan Airlines, Delta and Kenya Airways, and hundreds of other pairings. (Each airline will have information on its website about other carriers with which it partners.) You do not need to (nor can you) convert United miles into Lufthansa miles in order to take a Lufthansa flight.

It's very expensive to transfer miles between accounts. If you're eyeing a Delta award flight that costs 80,000 miles but you only have 60,000, getting a friend to transfer you 20,000 miles would incur an additional $230 in fees.

You can redeem your miles for someone else's flight. If you and your wife want an award flight, you don't each need the requisite number of miles. If you have 120,000 miles, you could book two 60,000 mile award flights.

Watch out for big fees on some award flights. It's important to do a bit of research before booking an award to see if there are expensive fuel surcharges attached to your "free" award flight. They're not common, but on some airlines and routes they can be hefty.

Unlike cash, miles are great for one-way international flights. When paying with cash, a one-way international flight is almost always significantly pricier than half a roundtrip flight. When redeeming miles, though, a one-way international flight is almost always half the cost of a roundtrip flight. Therefore, miles can be especially good value if you need a one-way international flight.

You don't earn miles on award flights. Nor are you eligible for complimentary upgrades.

Most miles come from credit cards, not flying. If you're wondering how people ever get enough miles for a free flight, this is usually how. Credit card sign-up bonuses can be incredibly lucrative, though it's a complex undertaking.

How Points Work

There are just a handful of financial institutions that award credit card points, some of which give them fancy names. These include Chase (Ultimate Rewards points), Citi (ThankYou points), American Express (Membership Rewards points), and Capital One.

As it relates to flights, there are two primary ways to use points: as a cash rebate (simple) or converting to airline miles for an award redemption (complex).

Let's walk through how you'd use Chase points as a cash rebate to book that $430 Vietnam flight. Once you've found a flight you want, the first step would be to log on to the Ultimate Rewards travel portal and make sure you can get the same price there. (In the unlikely event it's more expensive, try calling. Sometimes phone agents can access better fares than what show up online.) Next, you'll select your flights and Chase will tell you both the cash price and the points price. You can pay with either, or a combination of the two.

The value of the points—and thus how many you'd have to

use for the $430 flight—depends on what credit card you have. The more premium the card, the more value you receive from your Chase points. For example, if you have a Chase Freedom card, each point is worth 1 cent, so this Vietnam flight would cost 43,000 points. If instead you have the Chase Sapphire Reserve card, each point is worth 1.5 cents, meaning you'd need just 28,667 points for this flight.

Alternatively, you can convert points into miles, and redeem those for an award flight. The conversion rate is typically 1:1, though sometimes there are limited-time bonuses that offer, say, 30 percent more British Airways miles on any point conversions in a given month. Point conversions are free with credit cards aside from Amex, which charges a small fee.

Points are typically more valuable than miles because of their flexibility. Let's say you want a flight from Miami to Istanbul, returning from Dubai. When you search for award flights, though, the only availability is on United for the outbound and Emirates for the return. Not many people have Emirates miles stashed away, but if you have Chase points, you can convert a chunk to United and a chunk to Emirates, and get the award flight. If you had only United miles, you'd be stuck.

A few important items of background knowledge about points:

Not all points transfer to all mileage programs. Chase points can transfer to United but not Delta. Amex points can transfer to Delta but not United. The full list of possible transfers is ever changing; you can find the most up-to-date list online at bit.ly/pointstransfers.

You can transfer points to another person's account. The specific rules vary by program, but typically you can transfer your points to a family member.

You can pay with points for someone else's flight. You don't have to transfer points to someone else in order to book them a flight. Instead, you can use your points to book their flight. (Be aware: Selling your points or miles is barred.)

You can pay with points on almost all airlines. Each program varies slightly in which airlines show up in their search engine, but most airlines are available on most booking engines.

You can't undo points transfers. When you convert points to miles, it's a one-way ratchet. There's no way to reverse a transfer. That's why it's best to first find award availability—and ideally put an award on hold if you can—before you transfer.

You earn miles and are sometimes eligible to upgrade cabins on flights you paid for with points. Paying for a flight with points is akin to paying with cash, so the flight earns you miles and elite credit, and is sometimes eligible for upgrades. If you convert points to miles and use those miles to pay, you don't earn miles or elite credit, and it's not upgrade-eligible. (Convoluted, I know. Blame the banks and airlines.)

Should You Use Cash, Points, or Miles?

Let's consider that $430 roundtrip flight to Vietnam. Is it best to pay for it in cash, points, or miles?

- Paying with cash: $430
- Paying with miles: 70,000 miles
- Paying with points: 28,667 to 43,000 points

Right away we can cross paying with miles off the list. After all, if the cash price is $430, then you'd only be getting 0.6 cents per mile in value. Not good. Compare that with the fact that paying with points would cost anywhere from 43,000 to 28,667 points, depending on what credit card you had.

Whether it's better to pay with cash or points is more ambiguous. The benefit of paying in cash with a cheap fare like this is that it allows you to conserve your points for more valuable redemptions later. The benefit of paying in points is that it preserves your cash. You can't pay your rent in points, after all. The value someone places on their points vis-à-vis their cash will vary from person to person. If your wallet's feeling thin but you're points rich, there's nothing wrong with redeeming some for travel.

My advice: I wouldn't recommend paying with points if you're getting just 1 cent per point. You can get better value from your points by holding on to them for an award flight. If you have a credit card that gives you a higher redemption value, like Chase Sapphire Reserve, which inflates point values to 1.5 cents, then it can make sense to pay for flights with points, especially if you typically fly in economy.

In general, it's best to pay with cash or points in the following scenarios:

- **You found a cheap flight.** A $300 flight to Rome would cost $300, 20,000–30,000 points, or 60,000 miles. Eliminating miles is no question.
- **You have elite status.** You're sometimes eligible for complimentary upgrades and you earn miles faster if you have elite status. However, that's only true on flights you paid for with cash or points. If you redeemed miles for an award, you don't get these perks.
- **You can't find award availability for a flight you want.** The availability of award flights is highly variable, and blackout dates are common during peak travel periods. Don't assume a given flight you want has award availability.
- **You have a preference for simplicity.** Learning the nuances of points and miles isn't everyone's jam. Paying with cash or points is unquestionably simpler, and there's nothing wrong with preferring convenience.

In general, it's best to pay with miles (either miles you already have or miles you converted from points) in these scenarios:

- **No cheap flights are available.** This is more likely to be true if you live near a small airport (say, Fargo) or are flying to a small airport (say, Klaipeda). It's also often the case if you need a one-way international flight, as these tend to be pricey in cash. Of course, there would still need to be award availability.

- **There's an award flash sale.** In 2018, I woke up one morning and saw that Delta had put nonstop award flights from Portland to Amsterdam on sale. They normally cost 60,000 miles roundtrip, but for a brief time the price had been halved, to 30,000 miles. With the cash price at $1,000 for these flights, that meant I was getting 3.3 cents per mile in value, an excellent redemption. My wife and I quickly booked before the sale disappeared.
- **Business class redemptions.** If you're hoping for a business class flight, they're almost always prohibitively expensive when paying with cash. A normal business class flight from the United States to Asia costs somewhere in the neighborhood of $5,000, but you can get a business class award flight for 120,000 miles (a value of 4.16 cents per mile) without too much difficulty, and sometimes less than that.
- **If you have a ton of miles.** Airlines have a habit of devaluing miles over time, so long-term hoarding isn't a great idea. If you've got a stockpile and there's a decent-value award available for a trip you want, put those miles to work.

If it wasn't apparent, points and miles are an incredibly nuanced realm of the travel world. This chapter only scraped the surface of what's possible. There are people like The Points Guy who devote their entire careers to exploring how to get the most value possible from points and miles.

That doesn't mean you have to, though. You can get a ton of value from points and miles—especially if you take advantage of a flash sale or redeem miles for a premium seat—without having to know every detail or every possible award redemption.

What's more, miles are getting less valuable over time, at least for economy flights. A decade ago, when I first started getting serious about travel, cheap flights were rare. Sub-$300 roundtrip flights to Europe were unheard of, and even sub-$800 ones were scarce. In an era of expensive flights, miles were often a great value.

Nowadays, cheap flights have become so common that miles have lost much of their luster. If I expect to pay $900 for a flight to Vienna, then a 60,000-mile award flight is solid value. If I can get that same flight for $350, miles are terrible value.

Still, miles haven't become completely useless. There are times when they can get outsize value, especially if you're traveling through a small airport or you want to fly in the front of the plane. And at the end of the day, as much as I love cheap flights, there is perhaps one thing I love even more: free flights.

KEY TAKEAWAYS

- If you're traveling somewhere remote, two itineraries (the Greek Islands Trick) are usually cheaper than one. Book the cheapest long-haul flight you can find, and then pair it with a budget flight onward to your final destination.
- Booking two itineraries also allows you to build your own layover and see two places on a trip instead of one. Just be sure to put enough buffer time between

itineraries (ideally at least a day) so any delays won't cause you to miss the second flight.

- Know how the 24-hour rule works. It can be incredibly useful in a number of situations, from locking in a mistake fare to taking advantage of a price drop or better routing in a fare war.
- Don't count on cheap last-minute or standby flights popping up. Last-minute fares tend to skyrocket nowadays, although they're less likely to do so on budget airlines.
- Hidden-city ticketing can save money, but it's a complex strategy. Make sure you're familiar with how it works and its potential pitfalls before booking.
- Thanksgiving is both one of the most expensive times of year to fly domestically and one of the cheapest weeks of the year to fly internationally. It can be an especially convenient time to travel for families or people who have the week off work.
- Airline miles and credit card points can be a great value, but they're often complicated to use. For most people and most trips, the simplest route is just paying with points. In certain situations, like booking business class seats, using miles is the best approach.

CONCLUSION

I WAS IN MEXICO A FEW YEARS AGO, BOARDING A BUS TO A rural Oaxacan village where I learned Spanish and taught English. It was a long, bumpy ride, and I was hoping a seat would be free for the sixty-minute trek.

I sauntered past the driver and spotted an empty row second from the back. Yes! No more showing up to class with tired legs. As I picked up my pace and nearly made it to the seat, a guy sitting a few rows ahead tapped my arm and pointed toward the back.

"*Está ocupado.*"

Seat's taken.

I was confused because I thought the man said "It's occupied" but I could see it was empty. Maybe my Spanish wasn't as good as I'd thought?

"Gracias," I mumbled and walked a few more steps. And then I saw what he meant: Damned if there weren't two live turkeys sitting in the footrest, each cinched with cloth to form a carrying bag, like an upside-down babushka headscarf.

I looked at the villager sitting across the aisle. Was I really getting the Forrest Gump treatment? Her face made it clear: The turkeys were there first.

Calvin Trillin had a memorable line once, discussing the merits of eating iguana spleen: "The point is not to do it but to have done it."

I think about that often when I'm at home between vacations. Travel is wonderful, but it's easy to overlook travel's enduring gift of nostalgia. Ask anyone about their last vacation and their face will light up. They'll talk your ear off if given the opportunity, because the joy of a vacation doesn't end when we get home. We get to reminisce about past trips *for the rest of our lives*, whether it's finding a hidden waterfall or devouring an unforgettable pastry or just having a surprising run-in with turkeys.

The best memories aren't the ones you knew you were going to have. When you see the Eiffel Tower, it looks like it does in the photos. Maybe it's a touch bigger or smaller than expected, but it's generally as you thought it would be. It's still wonderful to see in person, of course, but in a funny way, photos do almost too good a job of portraying a place visually.

We're not nearly as adept at conveying other senses, though. That's where travel—being there, in person—truly excels. I saw photos of Murasawa steak before arriving in Japan, but nothing could truly prepare me for its butter-smooth taste. Nor could anyone have explained in advance the smell of drinking shot after shot of Boris Yeltsin–brand boxed vodka in a cramped Kyiv dining room. The sound of rustling palm fronds mixed with ocean waves, looking out on the Caribbean from an open-air Dominican cabaña.

The best memories are the unexpected ones, the experiences we couldn't anticipate. For me, it wasn't the tortoises that are seared in my memory of visiting the Galápagos but the way sea lions would swim right up to you while you're snorkeling. I don't remember much about the Seoul barbecue joints we popped in on, but I vividly remember the sound of thousands of Korean baseball fans cheering on their team—not by chanting, like Americans, but by singing. It's not the breweries in Germany I think back to, but that funny moment finding a love lock on a Frankfurt bridge with five names on it.

Travel is more than just an escape; the memories we develop, especially the surprising ones, are transformational. I've recounted them enough times that they've intertwined in my identity. Part of who I am today is the person who swam with sea lions in the Galápagos, sang with baseball fans in Korea, and laughed at polyamorous love locks in Germany.

Of course, a big part of my identity these days is also being a cheap flight expert, but I wasn't born that way. Like most people, I'd been taught for much of my life that flights were unaffordable. That dreaming about travel was great, but trying to do much of it before retirement was unrealistic.

Expensive flights are an incubation tank for excuses. They give us license to put off our travel goals. And for a while, I wasn't immune. I wanted to visit Europe, but flights seemed too expensive. I wanted to see Africa, but planning was hard. Asia sounded awesome, but who's got the time? At some point, though, I realized I could spend the rest of my life finding justifications for not traveling. Those excuses would do nothing to help me visit Japan or St. Lucia or Ireland.

When I landed my first job out of college in 2010, I was

getting paid $34,000 per year, less than half the median Washington, DC, salary. Nobody would've thought twice if I'd told them I couldn't afford to travel overseas.

But I didn't let an entry-level salary or the bewildering nature of flight prices stop me. I knew that the expense of flights was the one thing standing in my way; I took it as a challenge. If I could just solve the flights puzzle, everything else would fall into place. For the next few years, I dedicated myself to cracking the flights world. I was possessed, tortured by the knowledge that cheap flights were out there, yet I could never seem to find them.

Pretty soon, I started seeing some success. Roundtrip to Belgium for $225. Vietnam and Cambodia using miles. Business class to the Dominican Republic for free using a voucher from getting bumped. My coworkers, who knew how much money I made, were aghast. I was accused by multiple colleagues: "Do you have a secret trust fund?" How else could I take so many international trips?

But I wasn't a secret millionaire. I wore beat-up bowling shoes on the weekends and biked to work during snowstorms to save on subway fare. I tried explaining all the strategies I used. "The way I'm able to travel so much on a meager salary—and I want you to listen carefully here—is cheap flights," I repeated over and over, but it fell on deaf ears.

Over time, I began to realize that the reason my coworkers found it difficult to travel—and viewed me as a cheap flight whisperer—was that the way we search and plan our vacations is fundamentally broken. This book is my attempt to fix that misguided approach and ensure we all get a chance to see more of our world than we do today.

It's no stretch to say that cheap flights changed my life—three cheap flights in particular.

First, the $130 ticket to Milan. I remember it for the cannoli and wine and skiing, of course, but it was also the trip that prompted me to share my love of cheap flights with others. If that mistake fare had never popped up, would I have wound up pursuing a career as a flight expert? Who knows?

Second, a $200 flight to Puerto Rico. Not the best deal I've ever gotten, but it was special in another way. I didn't expect, sitting on Condado Beach watching the waves roll in, to meet someone life changing. With most people you meet on vacation, you don't imagine you'll ever see them again.

To my surprise we kept in touch—just as friends for a while, until that felt silly and not enough. Becoming a couple wasn't easy, though. We lived thousands of miles apart. And there were times the distance put a real strain on our ability to see a future together. The world is not lacking for long-distance relationships that fizzled because of too few visits.

The reason ours wasn't one of them: cheap flights. If I had paid full price for flights, I would've been lucky to visit once every five months. Instead, by using the strategies in this book—from flying out of cheaper nearby airports to leveraging flexibility on dates to booking well in advance to arbitraging Southwest's free cancellation policy—I was able to visit every five weeks. Goodbyes were far less painful because we knew the next trip was always around the corner.

That brings me to the third life-changing cheap flight: an award ticket to Hong Kong where, at 2 a.m., drenched in sweat from the hike up Victoria Peak, I asked that woman from the beach in Puerto Rico to marry me. Sure, we still would've gotten engaged even without the journey to Hong Kong (I hope!), but damn it would've been a lot less memorable.

I had no way of predicting the ensuing butterfly effect from that $130 Milan flight, and in a way that's one of the beauties of travel: You never know where it will take you. Not just the places you go, but the people you meet, the experiences you have, the person you become. We know travel is a transformational undertaking, but precisely *how* it will transform us is impossible to predict. That uncertainty isn't something to avoid, it's something to embrace. It's part of the fun.

For years, many of us have viewed travel as unrealistic because of costly flights. After all, there's a range of options with other aspects of travel—budget hotels and expensive hotels, world-class restaurants and street food, limousines and buses—but only one realistic way to cross an ocean: by airplane. There's no dingy motel or gas station sandwich that can make up for the expense of $1,500 Paris flights.

In the past decade, though, we've entered a new era of travel, all made possible by the drop in airfare. Travel is no longer just for the rich, because flights are no longer just for the rich. Cheap flights are real. They're spectacular. And their value comes not just from preserving some digits in your bank account, but from the way they open up the world.

Like Shanna in Bali and Lance in Rome, cheap flights let you visit bucket-list destinations you didn't think the whole family could afford. Like Josh in Croatia and Kristen in Hawaii, cheap flights let you accomplish travel goals you didn't even know you had. Like Chandra in France and Thomas in Morocco, cheap flights can let you live out a childhood dream.

In the end, though, flights are a means to an end. For all but us aviation geeks, flights just get us where we're going. The goal isn't luxury, it's just to not overpay.

Luckily, that's within our grasp. We can't control what the airlines charge, but we can control what we pay. The question isn't whether you can find cheap flights; it's whether you choose to take advantage of them.

ACKNOWLEDGMENTS

I couldn't have done this alone.

You'd think—as the founder of a company called Scott's Cheap Flights—that I would be excited to lap up personal recognition. But taking credit for others' effort is eminently uncomfortable for me, one reason (of many) I'd be a terrible celebrity.

This book is no different. There are so many who deserve recognition, and since I'd be a terrible celebrity, this is undoubtedly my one chance at an Oscars-style acceptance speech.

There is no world in which I don't give the first and most thanks to my wife and adventure partner, Anya, without whom this book (much less Scott's Cheap Flights) never would have happened. Thanks for letting me love you.

My daughter, Neko, who inspires me to sell her the world, whatever its failings.

My dad, Ralph, whose most generous gift was a love and appreciation for writing.

My mom, Muriel, who taught me the joy in finding a deal, and the freedom it can bring you.

My mother-in-law, Halyna, the world's best babushka.

My agent, Lindsay Edgecombe, who had a vision beyond my narrow pitch, and made this holistic.

My editor, Haley Swanson, whose patience and organization I can only aspire to one day possess.

My copy editor, Bob Castillo, whose ability to round a manuscript's hard edges is remarkable.

My co-founder, Brian Kidwell, who took a chance on a weird guy who claimed to love cheap flights.

The entire Scott's Cheap Flights team, whose credit unfairly funnels to me every time someone's cheap flight dream comes true.

Caroline Moss, whose story pitch on my worldwide trip was a true butterfly effect for my nascent cheap flight career.

Gary Leff, one of the few people I can unironically consider a "thought leader," for lending your expertise.

Khruangbin, whose dulcet tones kept my ears occupied throughout the manuscript.

And Reddit, my procrastination of choice, whose support and bullshit filter shaped the way I thought and talked about flights.

NOTES

INTRODUCTION

x *71 percent said airfare:* Morning Consult, "The State of American Travel 2018," accessed December 24, 2019, https://morningconsult.com/wp-content/uploads/2018 /06/MC-Brand-Intelligence-The-State-of-American-Travel -2018.pdf.

I: YOU DON'T TAKE ENOUGH VACATION: THE CURSE OF EXPENSIVE FLIGHTS

1 *top New Year's resolution:* Brenda Raftlova, "What Will Consumers Buy in 2020? Our Predictions," Offers.com, accessed December 24, 2019, https://www.offers.com /blog/post/new-year-purchase-predictions/.

1 *the #1 activity:* TD Ameritrade, "Redefining Aging," accessed December 24, 2019, https://s1.q4cdn.com /959385532/files/doc_downloads/research/2018/Aging -Survey.pdf.

1 *better ratings than sex:* Theresa Christine, "Young People Would Rather Travel Than Have Sex, Survey Finds," *Business Insider*, accessed April 15, 2020, https://www .businessinsider.com/what-people-would-give-up-travel -contiki-survey-2018-10.

1 *20 vacation days:* U.S. Travel Association, "State of Ameri-

can Vacation 2018," accessed December 24, 2019, https://www.ustravel.org/system/files/media_root/document/StateofAmericanVacation2018.pdf.

1 *A 2016 Airbnb poll:* Airbnb, "Airbnb and the Rise of Millennial Travel," accessed December 24, 2019, https://www.airbnbcitizen.com/wp-content/uploads/2016/08/MillennialReport.pdf.

2 *least vacation time:* U.S. Travel Association, "State of American Vacation 2018."

2 *or even zero:* U.S. Travel Association, "State of American Vacation 2018."

3 *felt the most stress:* John C. Crotts and Anita Zehrer, "An Exploratory Study of Vacation Stress," *Tourism Analysis* (2012), 547–552.

4 *uncertainty of planning:* Shawn Achor, "When a Vacation Reduces Stress—and When It Doesn't," *Harvard Business Review*, accessed December 24, 2019, https://hbr.org/2014/02/when-a-vacation-reduces-stress-and-when-it-doesnt.

5 *a 2019 survey:* U.S. Travel Association, "Travel Planning Fact Sheet (2019)," accessed June 21, 2020, https://www.ustravel.org/sites/default/files/media_root/document/TravelPlanning_Factsheet.pdf.

8 *"Losses hurt...":* Richard H. Thaler, "From Homo Economicus to Homo Sapiens," *Journal of Economic Perspectives* (2000), 133–141.

2: TRAVEL AS MEDICINE: HOW CHEAP FLIGHTS LEAD TO HAPPIER TRIPS (AND MORE OF THEM)

14 *93 million Americans:* National Travel & Tourism Office, "U.S. Citizen International Outbound Travel Up Six Percent in 2018," accessed December 24, 2019, https://travel.trade.gov/tinews/archive/tinews2019/20190402.asp.

14 *47 percent increase:* World Bank, "International tourism, number of departures—United States," accessed December 24, 2019, https://data.worldbank.org/indicator /ST.INT.DPRT?end=2017&locations=US&start=1995 &view=chart.

15 *A 2018 poll:* U.S. Travel Association, "State of American Vacation 2018."

16 *improves your mood:* Priceline, "New Survey from Priceline.com Unveils Travel Is Number One Mood Booster for Americans," *PR Newswire*, accessed December 24, 2019, https://www.prnewswire.com/news-releases/new-survey -from-pricelinecom-unveils-travel-is-number-one-mood-bo oster-for-americans-300285839.html.

16 *makes you more employable:* Lindsay Dogson, "More Than 80 Percent of Employers Think You're Better Suited for a Job If You've Been Travelling," *Business Insider*, accessed December 24, 2019, https://www.businessinsider.com/ travelling-make-you-more-employable-2017–6.

16 *lowers your risk:* Global Coalition on Aging, "Destination Healthy Aging: The Physical, Cognitive, and Social Benefits of Travel," accessed December 24, 2019, https://global coalitiononaging.com/wp-content/uploads/2018/07 /destination-healthy-aging-white-paper_final-web-1.pdf.

16 *A small percentage:* Qin Xie, "Revealed: Why Taking a Holiday REALLY Is Good for You with Hidden Benefits including Better Skin, Weight Loss and Even a Higher Sex Drive," *Daily Mail*, accessed December 24, 2019, https://www.dailymail.co.uk/travel/travel_news/article -3517543/Why-taking-holiday-REALLY-good-hidden -benefits-including-better-skin-weight-loss-higher-sex -drive.html.

16 *"As stress and anxiety decreases . . .":* Jordi Lippe-McGraw, "New Study Reveals Traveling Boosts Your Sex Life and

Can Help You Lose Weight," *Travel + Leisure*, accessed December 29, 2019, https://www.travelandleisure.com /travel-tips/offbeat/traveling-better-sex-life-weight-loss.

17 *"... promotes brain health ...":* Global Coalition on Aging, "Destination Healthy Aging."

17 *A 2010 study:* Thomas DeLeire and Ariel Kalil, "Does Consumption Buy Happiness? Evidence from the United States," *International Review of Economics* (2010), 163–176.

17 *We're far more likely:* Leaf Van Boven and Thomas Gilovich, "To Do or to Have? That Is the Question," *Journal of Personality and Social Psychology* (2003), 1193–1202.

18 *93 percent of travelers:* Global Coalition on Aging, "Destination Healthy Aging."

20 *In 2013, Dutch researchers:* Jessica de Bloom, Sabine A. E. Geurts, and Michiel A. J. Kompier, "Vacation (After-) Effects on Employee Health and Well-Being, and the Role of Vacation Activities, Experiences and Sleep," *Journal of Happiness Studies* (2013), 613–633.

21 *some surprising results:* Leif D. Nelson and Tom Meyvis, "Interrupted Consumption: Disrupting Adaptation to Hedonic Experiences," *Journal of Marketing Research* (2008), 654–664.

22 *loophole to hedonic adaptation:* Daniel Mochon, Michael I. Norton, and Dan Ariely, "Getting Off the Hedonic Treadmill, One Step at a Time: The Impact of Regular Religious Practice and Exercise on Well-Being," *Journal of Economic Psychology* (2008), 632–642.

22 *a seminal 2011 paper:* Elizabeth W. Dunn, Daniel T. Gilbert, and Timothy D. Wilson, "If Money Doesn't Make You Happy Then You Probably Aren't Spending It Right," *Journal of Consumer Psychology* (2011), 115–125.

5: THEN AND NOW: A BRIEF HISTORY OF HOW AIRLINES DETERMINE PRICES

73 *how airlines used to:* E. Mazareanu, "Net Profit of Commercial Airlines Worldwide from 2006 to 2020," *Statista*, accessed December 24, 2019, https://www.statista.com/statistics/232513/net-profit-of-commercial-airlines-world wide/.

73 *perverse arbitrage opportunity:* Tim Brady, *The American Aviation Experience: A History* (Carbondale: Southern Illinois University Press, 2001).

74 *diversifying their income:* Smithsonian National Air and Space Museum, "Who Flew?," *America By Air*, accessed D cember 24, 2019, https://airandspace.si.edu/exhibitions/america-by-air/online/innovation/innovation15.cfm.

75 *as one CAB member:* U.S. Congress, "Civil Aeronautics Act of 1938," Library of Congress, accessed December 24, 2019, https://www.loc.gov/law/help/statutes-at-large/75th-congress/session-3/c75s3ch601.pdf.

76 *CAB gave its blessing:* Harold A. Jones and Frederick Davis, "The Air Coach Experiment and National Air Transport Policy," *Journal of Air Law and Commerce* (1950), 1–21.

77 *"...[sleeping] berths, fully-reclining...":* "Multiple-Service Extended Overseas to Paris and Rome," *TWA Skyliner Magazine* (January 5, 1956), 1.

78 *Here's how airlines:* "Number of Scheduled Passengers Boarded by the Global Airline Industry from 2004 to 2020," *Statista*, accessed December 24, 2019, https://www.statista.com/statistics/564717/airline-industry-passenger-traffic-globally/.

79 *just 9 percent:* "Delta Air Lines: Evolving Sales Channels for Segmented Fare Offers," Centre for Aviation, accessed December 24, 2019, https://centreforaviation.com/analysis/reports/delta-air-lines-evolving-sales-channels-for-segmented-fare-offers-458157.

79 *Delta is not alone:* David Koenig, "United Courts the Well-Heeled with More Premium Seats," AP, accessed December 24, 2019, https://apnews.com/7d34c6a2366 c477ea563e70e26dd99c0.

80 *In 2018, American:* "American Airlines Group Reports Fourth-Quarter and Full-Year 2018 Profit," American Airlines, accessed December 24, 2019, https://americanairlines .gcs-web.com/news-releases/news-release-details/american -airlines-group-reports-fourth-quarter-and-full-year-3.

80 *$2 billion brought in:* Gary Leff, "Earnings Release: American Airlines Lost Money Flying Passengers Last Quarter," View from the Wing, accessed December 24, 2019, https:// viewfromthewing.com/earnings-release-american-air lines-lost-money-flying-passengers-last-quarter/.

80 *areas of revenue growth:* AnnaMaria Andriotis and David Benoit, "Sapphire Reserve Strains JPMorgan's Ties with United Airlines," *Wall Street Journal,* accessed December 24, 2019, https://www.wsj.com/articles/sapphire -reserve-strains-jpmorgans-ties-with-united-airlines-1156 1627802.

80 *According to Yahoo journalist:* Ethan Klapper, "More Than Meets the Eye," *Bluer Skies,* accessed June 18, 2020, https:// bluerskies.substack.com/p/more-than-meets-the-eye.

81 *secret corporate accounts:* Benjamin Mayo, "United Airlines Takes Down Poster That Revealed Apple Is Its Largest Corporate Spender," *9to5Mac,* accessed December 24, 2019, https://9to5mac.com/2019/01/14/united-airlines -apple-biggest-customer/.

82 *In 2018, U.S. airlines:* Bureau of Transportation Statistics, "Baggage Fees by Airline," Department of Transportation, accessed December 24, 2019, https://www.bts.gov /baggage-fees.

82 *additional $2.7 billion:* Bureau of Transportation Statis-

tics, "2018 Annual and 4th Quarter U.S. Airline Financial Data," Department of Transportation, accessed December 24, 2019, https://wwwbts.gov/newsroom/2018-annual -and-4th-quarter-us-airline-financial-data.

6: THE GOLDEN AGE OF CHEAP FLIGHTS: HOW AND WHY EVERYONE CAN NOW AFFORD TO FLY

87 *just $30:* "California Air Fares May Rise," *New York Times,* accessed December 24, 2019, https://www.nytimes .com/1979/02/26/archives/california-air-fares-may-rise -us-law-perils-states-control.html.

87 *In 1981, the average domestic:* Mark J. Perry, "Tuesday Afternoon Links," American Enterprise Institute, accessed December 24, 2019, https://www.aei.org/carpe-diem /tuesday-afternoon-links-23/.

87 *25 percent longer:* Mark J. Perry, "Wednesday Evening Links," American Enterprise Institute, accessed December 24, 2019, https://www.aei.org/carpe-diem/wednesday -evening-links-11/.

89 *half the rate of inflation:* "Airfares Are a Bargain," Airlines for America, accessed December 24, 2019, https://www .airlines.org/dataset/price-comparisons/.

90 *a Gallup poll found:* Andrew Dugan, "U.S. Fliers' Satisfaction with Ticket Prices Nosedives," Gallup, accessed December 24, 2019, https://news.gallup.com/poll/187952 /fliers-satisfaction-ticket-prices-nosedives.aspx.

90 *A 2018 Morning Consult poll:* Morning Consult, "State of American Travel 2018."

91 *most important factor driving their purchasing:* Samantha Shankman, "The 9 Factors Everyone Considers When Booking a Flight," Skift, accessed December 24, 2019, https://skift.com/2014/06/17/the-9-factors-everyone -considers-when-booking-a-flight/.

91 *on average fares drop:* Daniel M. Kasper and Darin Lee,

"An Assessment of Competition and Consumer Choice in Today's U.S. Airline Industry," Compass Lexecon, 2017.

92 *During the 2010s:* Kasper and Lee, "Assessment of Competition."

93 *Norwegian grew so quickly:* Sarah Young, "British Airways Loses New York Crown to Low-Cost Rival Norwegian," Reuters, accessed December 24, 2019, https://www.reuters.com/article/us-norweg-air-shut-british-airways-new-y/british-airways-loses-new-york-crown-to-low-cost-rival-norwegian-idUSKCN1MI1YE.

93 *In 1947, every New Yorker:* TWA, "Fly TWA to Geneva," Duke University Libraries Digital Repository, accessed December 24, 2019, https://repository.duke.edu/dc/ad access/T1980.

96 *four prominent Chinese airlines:* "Chinese Airlines Overtake US Carriers across the Pacific. The Big Dilemma: US-China Open Skies?," Centre for Aviation, accessed December 24, 2019, https://centreforaviation.com/anal ysis/reports/chinese-airlines-overtake-us-carriers-across-the-pacific-time-for-us-china-open-skies-222454.

96 *world's largest aviation market:* "Passenger Forecast," IATA, accessed December 24, 2019, https://airlines.iata.org/sites/default/files/p42-43%20DATA.pdf.

97 *In 1965, fewer than:* "Aviation: Come Fly with Me," accessed December 24, 2019, http://content.time.com/time/magazine/article/0,9171,833812,00.html.

97 *Fifty years later:* John P. Heimlich, "Status of Air Travel in the USA," Airlines for America, accessed December 24, 2019, https://www.airlines.org/wp-content/uploads/2016/04/2016Survey.pdf.

97 *in any given year:* "Airlines," Gallup, accessed December 24, 2019, https://news.gallup.com/poll/1579/Airlines.aspx.

7: UNPREDICTABLE AND IRRATIONAL: WHY AIRFARE IS SO VOLATILE

100 *A CheapAir.com analysis:* "Airfare Fluctuations: Can a Flight Price Really Change 135 Times?," CheapAir, accessed December 24, 2019, https://www.cheapair.com /blog/airfare-fluctuations-can-a-flight-price-really-change -135-times/.

101 *majority of fare changes:* Airfarewatchdog.com, "Confessions of an Airline Revenue Manager," Yahoo News (2014), accessed December 24, 2019, https://news.yahoo.com /confessions-airline-revenue-manager-094500117.html.

104 *Just 26 percent said:* Morning Consult, "State of American Travel 2018."

104 *"We do not sell . . .":* Will Horton, "Why Lufthansa Keeps First Class but Is Reconsidering Sandwich Catering," Runway Girl Network, accessed December 24, 2019, https:// runwaygirlnetwork.com/2019/07/04/why-lufthansa -keeps-first-class-but-is-reconsidering-sandwich-catering/.

8: THE FUNDAMENTALS: ANSWERS TO EVERYDAY FLIGHT-BOOKING QUESTIONS

134 *fatality odds are higher:* National Safety Council, "Injury Facts Chart: What Are the Odds of Dying From," accessed December 24, 2019, https://www.nsc.org/work-safety /tools-resources/injury-facts/chart.

142 *an IBM survey:* Michelle Higgins, "A Price to Pay When Skis Travel with You," *New York Times*, accessed December 24, 2019, https://www.nytimes.com/2008/12/07/travel /7pracbags.html.

9: CLEAR YOUR COOKIES: EIGHT FLIGHT-BOOKING MYTHS DEBUNKED

157 *"This is the one thing . . .":* Sophie-Claire Hoeller, "This Is the One Thing You Should Do When Searching for Flights Online," *Business Insider*, accessed December 24, 2019, https://www.businessinsider.com/clear-cooking-when -searching-for-flights-online-2015-9.

157 Time *magazine passed along:* Lucinda Shen, "Tricks to Snag the Best Flight Deal," *Time*, accessed December 24, 2019, https://time.com/4899508/flight-search-history -price/.

157 SmarterTravel*'s Ed Hewitt:* Ed Hewitt, "7 Mistakes to Avoid When Booking a Flight," SmarterTravel, accessed October 31, 2019, https://web.archive.org/web /20191031020934/https://www.smartertravel.com/7 -mistakes-avoid-booking-flight/.

158 *FareCompare claims:* Rick Seaney, "Cheapest Days to Fly and Best Time to Buy Airline Tickets," FareCompare, accessed December 24, 2019, https://www.farecompare .com/travel-advice/tips-from-air-travel-insiders/.

158 *Skyscanner says:* Emily Price, "This Is the Best Time to Book Flights in 2019," *Lifehacker*, accessed December 24, 2019, https://lifehacker.com/this-is-the-best-time-to -book-flights-in-2019-1831708590.

158 *Hopper argues anytime:* Anne Sraders, "Best Day of the Week to Book a Flight, According to Experts," TheStreet, accessed December 24, 2019, https://www.thestreet .com/personal-finance/savings/best-day-of-week-to -book-flight-14718627.

158 *Expedia swears:* "Expedia and ARC Make It Easier to Find the Cheapest Air Fares in 2018," *PR Newswire*, accessed December 24, 2019, https://www.prnewswire.com /news-releases/expedia-and-arc-make-it-easier-to-find -the-cheapest-air-fares-in-2018-663623453.html.

161 *they'd make more money:* Ken Littlewood, "Forecasting and Control of Passenger Bookings," *Journal of Revenue and Pricing Management* (2005), 111–123.

163 *a 20-hour trip:* TWA, "Yes, indeed . . . TWA's Family Budget Fares," Duke University Libraries Digital Repos-

itory, accessed December 24, 2019, https://repository
.duke.edu/dc/adaccess/T2021.

164 *Planes crashed constantly:* Richard Kebabjian, "Causes of
Fatal Accidents by Decade," PlaneCrashInfo.com, accessed
December 24, 2019, http://www.planecrashinfo.com
/cause.htm.

164 *being perpetually hijacked:* "Airline Hijackings 1945–
2015," Datagraver, accessed December 24, 2019, https://
www.datagraver.com/case/airline-hijackings-1945-2015.

164 *Minorities were not allowed:* Smithsonian National Air
and Space Museum, "Air Travel and Segregation," *America
By Air,* accessed December 24, 2019, https://airandspace
.si.edu/exhibitions/america-by-air/online/heyday/hey
day13.cfm.

164 *sexism and misogyny:* TWA, "TWA Air Hostess Quali-
fications," Duke University Libraries Digital Repository,
accessed December 24, 2019, https://repository.duke.edu
/dc/adaccess/T1960.

10: SHOULD YOU TAKE THAT TRIP? HOW TO THINK ABOUT OVERTOURISM AND EMISSIONS

165 *As of 2019:* Jocelyn Timperley, "Corsia: The UN's Plan
to 'Offset' Growth in Aviation Emissions after 2020,"
CarbonBrief, accessed March 28, 2020, https://www.car
bonbrief.org/corsia-un-plan-to-offset-growth-in-aviation
-emissions-after-2020.

166 *projected to double:* IATA, "Passenger Numbers to Hit
8.2bn by 2037," IATA, accessed March 28, 2020, https://
www.airlines.iata.org/news/passenger-numbers-to-hit
-82bn-by-2037-iata-report.

167 FiveThirtyEight *estimated:* Luke Jensen and Brian Yutko,
"Why Budget Airlines Could Soon Charge You to Use
the Bathroom," *FiveThirtyEight,* accessed March 28, 2020,

https://fivethirtyeight.com/features/if-everyone-went
-to-the-bathroom-before-boarding-the-plane-ticket-prices
-might-be-lower/.

170 *World Bank conducted a study:* Heinrich Bofinger and
Jon Strand, "Calculating the Carbon Footprint from
Different Classes of Air Travel," World Bank, accessed
March 28, 2020, http://documents.worldbank.org/curat
ed/en/141851468168853188/pdf/WPS6471.pdf.

170 *were the greenest:* Xinyi Sola Zheng, Brandon Graver,
and Dan Rutherford, "U.S. Domestic Airline Fuel Efficiency Ranking, 2017–2018," white paper (Washington,
DC: The International Council on Clean Transportation,
2019).

172 *"Collective action doesn't fall . . .":* Maria Bustillos, "Pascal's
Climate," *Popula*, accessed March 28, 2020, https://pop
ula.com/2019/03/03/pascals-climate/.

172 New York Magazine*'s:* Eric Levitz, "You Can't Save the
Climate by Shrinking Your Carbon Footprint," *New York
Magazine*, accessed March 28, 2020, https://nymag.com
/intelligencer/2019/02/bernie-sanderss-private-plane
-rides-dont-matter.html.

172 *"Living in the world . . .":* Alexandria Ocasio-Cortez, Twitter, accessed March 28, 2020, https://twitter.com/AOC
/status/1102021054363586561.

173 *"At first, I thought . . .":* Taylor Kubota, "Stanford Graduate
Student Finds That Emphasizing Individual Solutions to
Big Issues Can Reduce Support for Government Efforts,"
Stanford News Service, accessed March 28, 2020, https://
news.stanford.edu/press-releases/2017/06/12/emphasiz
ing-indivernment-efforts/.

174 *2019 ProPublica investigation:* Lisa Song, "An Even More
Inconvenient Truth: Why Carbon Credits for Forest
Preservation May Be Worse Than Nothing," ProPublica,

accessed March 28, 2020, https://features.propublica.org
/brazil-carbon-offsets/inconvenient-truth-carbon-credits
-dont-work-deforestation-redd-acre-cambodia/.

175 *only one in ten Americans:* Negar Ballard, "Most Americans
Who Believe Their Personal Emissions Have an Impact
on Climate Change Say They Are Familiar with Carbon
Offsetting, Though Most Don't Know Exactly What It Is,"
Ipsos, accessed March 28, 2020, https://www.ipsos.com
/en-us/news-polls/Two-Thirds-of-Americans-Say-They
-Are-Familiar-with-Carbon-Offsetting-Though-Most
-Don%E2%80%99t-Know-Exactly-What-It-Is.

176 *proclaimed* The Atlantic: Annie Lowrey, "Too Many People Want to Travel," *The Atlantic,* accessed March 28,
2020,   https://www.theatlantic.com/ideas/archive/2019
/06/crowds-tourists-are-ruining-popular-destinations
/590767/.

176 *"The accessible price . . .":* Leonid Bershidsky, "Prepare for
Another Summer of Overtourism," *Bloomberg,* accessed December 24, 2019, https://www.bloomberg.com/opinion
/articles/2019-06-09/europe-s-top-vacation-sites-need
-options-to-fight-overcrowding.

178 *"Save the elephants? . . .":* Costas Christ, "What If All
That Flying Is Good for the Planet?," *New York Times,*
accessed December 24, 2019, https://www.nytimes
.com/2019/11/19/opinion/climate-change-travel.html.

II: THE UNEXPECTED JOYS OF TRAVEL: HOW TO GET BETTER AT VACATIONING

184 *The study found that:* Chris Ryan, "The Travel Career Lad-
der: An Appraisal" *Annals of Tourism Research* (1998),
936–957.

184 *Not all travel pros:* Philip L. Pearce, *Tourist Behaviour: Themes
and Conceptual Schemes* (Bristol, UK: Channel View Publications, 2005).

185 *the following scenario:* Daniel Kahneman and Dale T. Miller, "Norm Theory: Comparing Reality to Its Alternatives," *Psychological Review* (1986), 136–153.

186 *"Suppose their decisions . . .":* Thomas Gilovich and Victoria Husted Medvec, "The Temporal Pattern to the Experience of Regret," *Journal of Personality and Social Psychology* (1994), 357–365.

188 *my father once wrote:* Ralph Keyes, *Second Thoughts: The Power of Positive Regret* (David Scott Publishers, 2014).

189 *The first group:* Terence R. Mitchell, Leigh Thompson, Erika Peterson, and Randy Cronk, "Temporal Adjustments in the Evaluation of Events: The 'Rosy View,'" *Journal of Experimental Social Psychology* (1997), 421–448.

190 *In 2010, Dutch researchers:* Jeroen Nawijn, Miquelle A. Marchand, Ruut Veenhoven, and Ad J. Vingerhoets, "Vacationers Happier, but Most not Happier After a Holiday," *Applied Research in Quality of Life* (2010), 35–47.

191 *people will pay more:* George Loewenstein, "Anticipation and the Valuation of Delayed Consumption," *Economic Journal* (1987), 666–684.

191 *"Consumers derive value . . .":* Amit Kumar, Matthew A. Killingsworth, and Thomas Gilovich, "Waiting for Merlot: Anticipatory Consumption of Experiential and Material Purchases," *Psychological Science* (2014), 1924–1931.

192 *planners were more likely:* U.S. Travel Association, "State of American Vacation 2018."

194 *according to a poll:* U.S. Travel Association, "Travel Planning Fact Sheet (2019)."

195 *next highest response:* Mitchell et al., "Temporal Adjustments in the Evaluation of Events."

196 *"Vacations continue to provide . . .":* Jesse Singal, "How to Maximize Your Vacation Happiness," *New York Magazine*, accessed December 24, 2019, https://www.the

cut.com/2015/07/how-to-maximize-your-vacation
-happiness.html.

198 "... *very, very important.*": TED Talk, "The Riddle of
Experience vs. Memory | Daniel Kahneman," YouTube,
accessed December 24, 2019, https://www.youtube.com
/watch?v=XgRlrBl-7Yg.

198 "*That [way] we wouldn't ...*": TED Radio Hour, "How Do
Experiences Become Memories?," NPR, accessed December
24, 2019, https://www.npr.org/2013/11/29/182676143
/how-do-experiences-become-memories.

12: PRO TIPS: ADVANCED FLIGHT-BOOKING TACTICS TO MAXIMIZE YOUR VACATION

223 "*After a ticket ...*": "Guidance on the 24-Hour Reservation Requirement," Department of Transportation, accessed December 24, 2019, https://www.transportation
.gov/sites/dot.gov/files/docs/Notice_24hour_hold_final
20130530.pdf.

225 "*airlines may cancel ...*": "Buying a Ticket," Department of
Transportation, Aviation Consumer Protection, accessed
December 24, 2019, https://www.transportation.gov
/individuals/aviation-consumer-protection/buying-ticket.

227 *But with airlines like People Express:* Eric Schmitt, "The
Art of Devising Air Fares," *New York Times*, accessed December 24, 2019, https://www.nytimes.com/1987/03/04
/business/the-art-of-devising-air-fares.html.

232 *When consumers buy:* Chuck Klosterman, "Paying for a
Need for Speed," *New York Times*, accessed December 24,
2019, https://www.nytimes.com/2014/09/14/magazine
/paying-for-a-need-for-speed.html?_r=0.

235 *a 2017 poll:* Morning Consult, "U.S. Travel Association
Polling Presentation," U.S. Travel Association, accessed December 24, 2019, https://www.ustravel.org/sites/default
/files/media_root/document/MC-Poll-Slides-V3.pdf.

235 least *popular months:* Bureau of Transportation Statistics, "Load Factor," Department of Transportation, accessed December 24, 2019, https://www.transtats.bts.gov/Data_Elements.aspx?Data=5.

INDEX

ABOUT THE AUTHOR

Scott Keyes is the founder of Scott's Cheap Flights, a travel platform with more than two million members around the world. It's been called "the travel world's best-kept secret" by *Thrillist* and received praise in the *New York Times* and *Washington Post*, among others. Prior to becoming a leading expert on cheap flights, Scott graduated from Stanford University and worked for years as a journalist, with bylines in the *Washington Post*, *The Atlantic*, *The Guardian*, *The Nation*, and other publications. When he's not on a plane, he lives with his wife and daughter in Portland, Oregon.